An Educator's Guide to Block Scheduling

Related Titles of Interest

New Kids on the Net: Internet Activities in Secondary Mathematics
Sheryl Burgstahler and Christine Murakami
ISBN: 0-205-28593-7

New Kids on the Net: Internet Activities in Secondary Science
Sheryl Burgstahler and Kurt Sahl
ISBN: 0-205-28594-5

Quantum Teaching: Orchestrating Student Success
Bobbi DePorter, Mark Reardon, and Sarah Singer-Nourie
ISBN: 0-205-28664-X

Bringing the Social Sciences Alive: Simulations for Politics, History, Economics, and Government
Frederick M. Hess
ISBN: 0-205-28170-2

Teaching Writing in Middle and Secondary Schools: Theory, Research, and Practice
Margot Iris Soven
ISBN: 0-205-18897-4

■ An Educator's Guide to Block Scheduling

Decision Making,

Curriculum Design, and

Lesson Planning Strategies

Mary M. Bevevino
Dawn M. Snodgrass
Kenneth M. Adams
Joan A. Dengel

Edinboro University

Allyn and Bacon
Boston • London • Toronto • Sydney • Tokyo • Singapore

Series editor: Frances Helland
Series editorial assistant: Bridget Keane
Marketing manager: Anne Morrison
Manufacturing buyer: Suzanne Lareau

Library of Congress Cataloging-in-Publication Data

An educator's guide to block scheduling : decision making, curriculum
   design, and lesson planning strategies / Mary M. Bevevino . . . [et
   al.].
       p. cm.
   Includes bibliographical references (p.   ) and index.
   ISBN 0-205-27847-7
     1. Block scheduling (Education)   2. Curriculum planning.
   3. Lesson planning.   I. Bevevino, Mary M.
   LB3032.2.E38   1998
   371.2′42—dc21   98-14869
                                                                          CIP

Printed in the United States of America
10 9 8 7 6 5 4 3 2 1   02 01 00 99 98

For
Dick, Erin, Eric, and Michele from MMB
Buck and Taylor, Mom and Dad from DMS
Ann, Tony, and Nick from KMA
Ray and Michael from JAD

■ Contents

■ Preface

An Educator's Guide to Block Scheduling: Decision Making, Curriculum Design, and Lesson Planning Strategies is a book for teachers in middle school and secondary classrooms, for middle and high school administrators, for preservice teachers preparing for a career in education, and for other educators interested in expanding knowledge of the extended-block schedule and the techniques that are most effective for teaching in extended-block configurations. This practical text is useful as a resource book and as an easy-to-use desk reference. For teachers and administrators with limited or no experience using an extended-block schedule, beginning with Part One may be most helpful. Those people with experience in the block schedule may wish to begin with the content-specific chapters and refer to Part One for review.

The straightforward approach of the text explains several extended-block schedules and a variety of strategies across academic curriculum areas to make the most of what these schedules offer teachers and students. Examples shared by teachers operating within the block schedule are provided throughout the book to demonstrate clearly each of the strategies examined. Fully developed lesson plans provided by classroom teachers, preservice teachers, and university faculty in multiple curriculum areas are also included. Although the book contains content-specific chapters, strategies presented are not limited to one specific discipline and are flexible enough to be used across curriculum areas. Information is provided in a manner that is comfortable for those who are only beginning to investigate this new use of time as well as those who are already engaged in teaching with longer periods of time.

■ Acknowledgments

We are grateful to our editor, Frances Helland, for her expert guidance and support. We also thank Buck Snodgrass for his photography skills in capturing the extended-block schedule in action. Thank you, also, to the General McLane School District for generously opening their building, to their teachers for allowing us to interrupt their school days, and to their students for participating in our photographs.

We appreciate the advice and support given by Rick Scaletta and by our reviewers, Amy M. Mulligan, Northwestern Senior High School, Albion, PA; Candace A. Kemp, General McLane School District, Edinboro, PA; and Irwin Ozer, Richardson Independent School District, Richardson, TX. For their technical support, we would also like to thank Melissa Oswalt, Lynette Osterberg, and Nathan Bushyager. Finally, we give special thanks to all of the teachers and preservice teachers who submitted lesson plans for inclusion in this book.

An Educator's Guide to Block Scheduling

■ PART ONE

The extended block gives department members time to coordinate curriculum and share strategies.

■ 1
Considering the Block

WE WERE SITTING in the teachers' room ready to analyze areas for improvement with Lisa's current student teacher when I commented that the student was lucky to be working with Lisa as her mentor teacher and also on the extended-block schedule.

Lisa laughed. "I know you remember that I was one of the teachers who didn't want to change when we voted to try the block two years ago."

"I do remember your comments in those initial meetings. What was your biggest fear about switching?" I asked.

"What concerned me most was time. I couldn't see how I could do my job with fewer minutes. I just looked at 50 minutes times 180 days versus 90 minutes times 90 days, and it was easy to see that I'd have fewer contact minutes on the block. I figured no matter which form of extended schedule we picked, adjustments would need to be made for lost minutes. I was afraid my students would lose out with the switch.

"Of course, I wasn't thinking of the time spent introducing, reviewing, and closing each of my 50-minute classes, the lack of time to do in-depth analysis, and the fact that several times a year, my classes would be cut out of the schedule for assemblies, pep rallies, or activity period. That doesn't happen now, by the way. We take five minutes from each of the four blocks, add that to the 25 minutes set aside for tutorial each day, and create an assembly time or an activity period."

"You seem so enthusiastic now," the student teacher pointed out. "Why the changes?"

Lisa paused, remembering. "We were lucky. Our administration gave us a year to prepare for the change. In our department, we used the national standards, our state guidelines, our own curriculum guide, and our scope and sequence. We began by asking ourselves what we wanted our students to know and to be able to do when they finished each of our courses that they didn't know or couldn't do when they walked in the door at the beginning of each course. Then, we analyzed what each of us covered.

"What came out of those meetings was a leaner curriculum. We cut overlap and overall fat in favor of addressing each concept in more depth. We were also given planning time in the summer, and I spent it getting the first month's lessons lined up. I can see why some teachers fail when their schools try to move to the block. If the school district doesn't invest the time and effort to educate their teachers, students, and even parents, and if they don't give teachers time and training, how can those teachers hope to be effective in a teaching schedule none of them have ever experienced? Change is hard! People need to be receptive first, then willing, and finally prepared."

"You said something about the American Dream yesterday. You said I'd soon be able to see what you mean by more depth and by your intention to guide students to greater understanding. Can you explain that?" her student teacher asked.

"That's a good one to use as an example. I used to assign five novels over the course of the year that specifically explored the American Dream, a big deal in

American literature. Now I assign three, but I plan differently. Before we started the block, we had several inservice meetings on constructivist learning, inquiry strategies, and teaching with cooperative learning designs and learning stations—which I hadn't really considered before. So I set up a series of learning stations based on the topic of the American Dream. In the first one, the students have to analyze their own concept of success. We have a number of English as a Second Language students here, and they have different opinions about success in America than a lot of my other students, so that individual analysis is followed by comparison with other students' goals and dreams.

"In another station, they compare their own dream of success with those of the characters from three of the novels we've read. They also look at American art and connect their own experiences and dreams with what they see depicted by famous artists. What they come out of all of this with, I think, is a concept of the American Dream based on their own prior experiences and their future goals. They develop a deeper understanding of what Americans have considered as the American Dream through literature, history, and art.

"In my previous classes of 50 minutes, I defined the concept and we discussed its importance to the novels and the characters. I treated five novels in a more superficial way. I covered them. With this approach, I'm creating the setting for much deeper insight."

She added with a smile, "I protested in the beginning. Now, I don't think I could give this up! I might just have to look for another job if we were to revert back to the seven-period day."

Lisa's comments reinforced the reaction of many teachers now involved with extended-block scheduling.

Looking at time is the most recent of the alternatives to traditional education in two decades of educational reform. We see the move to extended-block scheduling as revolutionary for the American school system and also as a relatively simple way to encourage the implementation of innovative teaching strategies presented to us in recent years. As far back as 1983, *A Nation at Risk* (National Commission on Excellence in Education, 1983) listed time as an area of concern for administrators and teachers. Time issues were identified as ineffective use of class time, too little meaningful homework time, and too little time devoted to the development of good study skills.

This report also recommended that currently available school time be restructured for more effective utilization and that schools consider adding more time to the current school day or to the yearly academic calendar, creating more concentrated time for the learning of core subjects. Some of us have experienced the shift to the eight-period day or to the longer school year, but generally, use of time has received the least amount of attention in the list of suggestions put forth in *A Nation at Risk*.

Instead of concentrating on the recommendations regarding the use of time, throughout the 1980s, administrators and teachers planned and implemented changes in both curriculum and instructional strategies. Most of us attended inservice meetings or workshops in cooperative learning, in learning styles, and in student-active learning environments and approaches; time and scheduling, however, were not a major focus for change. We learned interesting approaches to teaching and learning, but most of us were already so frustrated by large student loads, multiple preparations, and little time even to breathe that we had no energy left to plan anything new. Besides, many of the cooperative learning and inquiry-based approaches seemed to require more time; time we didn't have.

In the 1990s we are being asked to analyze our teaching effectiveness related to time. In 1994 the National Commission on Time and Learning published *Prisoners of Time,* an investigation of the issue of time and instructional effectiveness in U.S. schools. This report focused on factors related to time in the nation's schools as well as on traditional inhibitors of academic improvement. The commission identified four important time-bound factors:

1. The typical number of days of school required by law is 180 days per year.
2. Most schools provide only 5.6 hours of actual class time per day.
3. All schools base requirements for graduation on Carnegie units.
4. Regardless of the subject matter, each class has an equal time slot, an average of 51 minutes (National Commission on Time and Learning, 1994).

The commission also identified five inhibitors of academic improvement:

1. The fixed clock and calendar is a fundamental design flaw that must be changed.
2. Academic time has been stolen to make room for a host of nonacademic activities.
3. Today's school schedule must be modified to respond to the great changes that have reshaped American life outside school.
4. Educators do not have the time they need to do their job properly.
5. Mastering world-class standards will require more time for almost all students.

Many schools have not addressed the commission's concerns. As of 1994, however, Cawelti reported that 39% of U.S. high schools had moved to the extended-block schedule or planned to do so by 1994 (Hackmann, 1995).

Increasingly, the American public favors increased time, especially by adding to the academic yearly calendar (National Commission on Time and Learning, 1994). The report also revealed that U.S. schools were asking students to learn the same amount of academic content as students in other countries, but in less concentrated time, sometimes in only half the time. In addition, other countries were shown to have higher expectations and standards and to hold education in higher esteem than the United States. Educational institutions in countries such as Japan and Germany have been shown to demand twice as much core subject content as American schools.

It is with these comparisons and conditions in mind that *Prisoners of Time* (1994) proposed the use of extended-block scheduling as a vehicle for the implementation of more flexible use of time. This study asked us to encourage the use of a variety of teaching methods and emphasized the recommendation that scheduling and adjustments to time use in schools be done with the needs of the students in mind.

RATIONALE FOR ALTERNATIVE SCHEDULING

Alternative scheduling has been described by Canady and Rettig (1995) as a time management strategy that addresses the enhancement of quality time, the building of a school climate, and the provision of a variety of learning time frames.

Because of its recent implementation, the impact of alternative scheduling has yet to be validated by a firm empirical research base. Hottenstein (1998, p. 119) calls for "longitudinal studies of all forms of block scheduling across America on an ongoing, consistent basis." However, assessment to date has revealed that several areas, including school climate, student learning, and teaching environment, appear to improve with the move to alternative scheduling.

The School Climate

The extended time block creates a better school climate overall by giving time for in-depth learning activities, with more opportunities for collaborative learning, authentic learning experiences, and student-active classrooms (Canady & Rettig, 1995). Instruction also can include more integrated and interdisciplinary curriculum units. Students and teachers are not limited as rigidly to the four walls of the classroom; the longer block of time allows for investigations and experiences outside the traditional setting.

Student Learning

Extended scheduling provides more time for student–teacher interaction. If we have fewer students per term and consequently less paperwork, we can structure questions requiring more in-depth responses in class discussions and on written tasks. In class discussions, more accountability is placed on individual students to interact. Those average students who tended to remain invisible with the traditional schedule have increased opportunities to interact with teachers (Hackmann, 1995). Fewer class changes per day have resulted in an added bonus: a decrease in discipline problems and a more serious learning environment. On a personal level, many of us involved in the extended-block schedule have discovered that we know our students better than we did within the traditional configuration.

A more positive school climate and more in-depth learning opportunities are complemented by an increase in the number of courses that a student is able to complete within the four years of high school. With some models of alternative scheduling, students can come to the second semester of the senior year with all requirements completed. With a semester block of time available, they may wish to pursue career training, work-site experience, more advanced courses in areas of interest, or even college classes. The options also exist to initiate technical training and/or to pursue associate degree programs in postsecondary institutions (Edwards, 1995). In addition, the increased time available for more educational opportunities permits the inclusion of instruction in the fine arts, computer skills, family living, and consumer education.

The Teaching Environment

As secondary schools move toward the various extended-block schedules, we as teachers have more time to prepare for our classes because the number of assigned classes is fewer.

"After fifteen years teaching three preparations a day in American history, sociology, and economics, I felt I had lost that edge. I've always considered myself a conscientious teacher, so I did try to include some of the new strategies that I picked up from workshops. But with three preps, 170 students, and six classes a day, I just didn't have anything left for extra planning, for doing something different," Mr. Z explained.

"But now it's different. I still teach the same courses each year, but I have American history and government in the fall, and American history and sociology in the spring. Plus, I teach three blocks of 90 minutes a day with about 90 students each semester. That and the longer prep time have given me a new lease on life. And I've added activities that I couldn't do before, critical thinking exercises, some learning cycles. I have time to find out about kids. The whole thing has been good for me, and so it's good for my students, too."

In addition, administrators have been encouraged to see that the extended preparation time engenders increased collaboration by giving the teaching staff opportunities to share materials and ideas. Having fewer classes and fewer students per term allows more in-depth preparation and experimenting with the planning and implementation of complex learning methods. Because there is less need to repeat material for seven periods a day and less repetition of housekeeping duties such as taking roll and making announcements, teachers feel less stress and pressure. We have more time to breathe, allowing ideas to flow and often experiencing an exciting sense of rejuvenation as well.

SUCCESS WITH THE EXTENDED-BLOCK SCHEDULE

Teachers throughout the country have responded positively to the various extended-block scheduling formats. At Hope High School in Hope, Arkansas, the intensive schedule caused teachers to discover that they could carry out the teaching of a total concept in one class session (Wilson, 1995). In Hatboro-Horsham High School in Pennsylvania, teachers began to use newer teaching methods, were far more creative, and had more time to interact meaningfully with individual students (Hottenstein & Malatesta, 1993). Edwards (1995) found similar results when studying the Orange County, Virginia, High School; 88 percent of teachers expressed approval of intensive scheduling after one semester on the new time schedule, and expressed similar views at the end of the year.

To date, the extended-block schedule is still aligned with the Carnegie unit; however, teachers complete an entire course in one semester and teach fewer classes per day (Needham, 1993). The alternative schedule encourages in-depth learning experiences and promotes higher levels of learning and internalization of concepts.

Studies show that students also respond favorably to the extended-block schedule. When asked about the shift in time management at his high school, Jason, a senior, explained: "In my ninth-grade year, we were still on the regular schedule. I had homework from seven classes every night, so I picked the ones I thought were more important and did those. We went to the block in tenth grade. Now I have four subjects to do in a semester instead, and I concentrate on the four a lot more than I did on seven. Plus, it's a lot like college. I'm responsible for learning the stuff in one semester and get to move on to study other things the next term. It's pretty cool."

Students cited a more relaxed schedule, more personal one-to-one time with teachers, and more time in class to practice what they are taught (Needham, 1993). Concentrating on fewer subjects at a time appears to help struggling students (Hottenstein & Malatesta, 1993).

As administrators and teachers, those of us considering the block worry about less retention of content and decline in achievement. Two studies by Bateson (1990) and Marshall, Taylor, Bateson, and Brigden (1995) do indicate that districts need to be concerned about achievement. They point to data from *The British Columbia Assessment of Mathematics and Science,* which has shown a decline in achievement scores (Kramer, 1997). Results from a study of North Carolina high schools (Averett, 1994), however, show no negative effect on student achievement. Other studies are appearing that show no decline in achievement, and schools report that grade point averages have not declined, and in some instances have increased. As a result of Orange County, Virginia, High School's initiation of the 4 × 4 block in 1993, Edwards (1995) reports that more students are taking and passing the Advanced Placement exams. Grades have improved at Orange County High as well. At Skyline High School in Longmont, Colorado, students who are participating in the trimester extended block are also earning better grades overall (Stumpf, 1995). At Wasson High School in Colorado Springs, more students are achieving honor-roll status. Students at Orange County High School in Virginia are earning more credits over a four-year high school experience and are taking more courses in areas such as mathematics, science, foreign languages, social studies, and English. In addition, those students who do fail a course have twice as many opportunities to reschedule that subject during the four-year span. The extended block, then, can provide the opportunity to increase our expectations of students and to allow them to schedule additional courses during their high school careers.

Considerations

Stakeholders in a school district should consider the following points as they begin the discussion about change.

- A change to alternative scheduling needs to be considered carefully by all of us before the move is made.
- Administrators and teachers need time to learn about the block and to develop approaches best suited to their districts.
- Staff development is crucial to the success of the extended-block schedule.
- Through careful preparation and student-active planning, teachers can be more positive about potential success with low-risk activities that add to the variety of teaching strategies necessary to sustain student attention during the extended time period.
- Preliminary planning needs to include the formation of additional course offerings designed to take students to higher levels of learning beyond the current expectations.
- Parents and students need to be involved in planning for the move to the extended block.
- Parent education and community information need to be integral parts of administrative planning. Parents need to understand the benefits that this change can bring to their children and the part they can play in guiding their children to higher expectations.

The school district that ignores this crucial planning may not succeed with the new time schedule.

If teachers do not have a voice in the change, they may not support the new schedule by altering their teaching practices to include student-active, in-depth lessons. Even if they agree with the change to the block, if they do not have adequate planning time allotted before and after the move, they may not have experienced adequate inservice preparation in alternative teaching approaches to implement student-active strategies successfully. Should that happen, students may find themselves in classes taught in exactly the same way as before, with extended "homework" time within the class period. Teachers need time to reflect on their course offerings and to decide on meaningful homework assignments. With the extended-block schedule, all faculty must rethink every lesson they teach. With change comes a sense of disequilibrium that can be addressed through initial inservice programs and continuing inservicing after the block has been implemented. "Models of successful teaching behaviors, instructional methods, and management techniques should be emphasized" (Hamdy & Urich, 1998, p. 82). Other educational reforms may allow teachers to pick and choose (or totally neglect) new techniques, but changing to the extended block is systemic (Scaletta, 1997, personal communication).

If a district does not require students to take additional courses or to use the final semester for initial two-year or four-year post–high school preparation, or if it fails to give teachers time to plan additional offerings, that district may find that students have finished their state requirements by the first semester of their senior year and are not choosing to pursue more challenging course offerings, or are not beginning their post–high school preparation during that final term.

In such a district, students may feel they can just space out requirements with electives in such a way that they have only two courses to complete during their final semester and have the right to leave in the middle of the day. If allowed to manipulate the system in this way, students may avoid scheduling more math, English, social studies, science, foreign language, creative arts, or vocational training. Such a result would thwart one of the extended block's advantages: the opportunity to raise expectations of our students.

Parents who are not part of the decision-making process may choose, in the worst-case scenario, to subvert the move to the block. Those parents who support the move still may not understand their potential role in guiding their child to take the best advantage of new course offerings or opportunities offered by local post–high school technical training or early admission to area four-year colleges. Considering these crucial stakeholders will add to the potential for success in a move to the extended-block schedule.

This book is designed for administrators and teachers who are considering the change to block scheduling or who have already done so and seek suggestions for planning lessons. Part One presents a variety of extended-block models and provides a format for decision making. Administrators and staff can utilize the evaluation rubrics for curriculum, instructional methods, resource allocation, contractual obligations, and assessment to analyze their district's unique needs and to decide which format will serve their students best. This format provides opportunity for stakeholders in each school to be involved in the decision-making process. Part One also presents the crucial elements of cooperative learning and inquiry design and study skills development, with suggestions for implementation within the extended block.

Part Two presents four content-specific chapters, which help English, science, social studies, and mathematics teachers to analyze their specific needs. Each chapter presents lesson plan models designed to help them redesign their teaching strategies for maximum learning potential within the block. Teachers will find the national standards for the content area addressed, the use of cooperative learning and inquiry-based planning discussed, and specific suggestions for implementation of model plans presented for their consideration.

Part Three includes sample plans created by teachers currently working in school districts utilizing the extended-block schedule or by advanced undergraduate education majors planning for extended-block lessons. These include core curriculum plans in English, social studies, science, and mathematics, as well as samples from the areas of career planning, child development, family and consumer science, German, geography, and Spanish.

Districts that attempt to change to an extended-block format without allowing time and training for teachers may be paving the way for failure. Any reinvention of time should be made carefully and with the input of all stakeholders in a school district:

- Administrators
- Teachers
- Students
- Parents

Then, our own enthusiasm, the willingness of teachers to reevaluate curriculum and to include new approaches to learning, the provision of time for staff development, and community support can pave the way for a successful move to the extended-block schedule.

■ 2

Examining Models
and Making Decisions

AS YOU BEGIN to consider the adoption of intensive scheduling for your school, several important considerations should be made by all stakeholders in the school and community. Before adopting any particular model, gather information from as many schools as possible. Review the different models as you see their individual application to your school. Although considerable similarities exist between and among school districts across the nation in terms of curriculum, instructional practice, contractual obligations, human and capital resource allocations, and performance assessment, the unique way in which these broad variables contribute to the process of change at the local level requires that each school district carefully analyze the independent and collective impact of those variables within their own schools.

"Only in the last decade have educators begun to capitalize on the potential of scheduling to improve schools" (Canady & Rettig, 1995, p. 10). Much can be learned from those who have moved through the planning process toward the implementation of intensive scheduling. One of the lessons grounded in experience that can direct these deliberations is offered by Donald Hackmann (1995, pp. 24–27):

- Employ a systems thinking approach.
- Secure the support of your superiors.
- Understand the change process.
- Involve all stakeholders.
- Brainstorm creative alternatives.
- Examine the budgetary implications.
- Plan faculty inservices.
- Include an evaluation component.
- Share and celebrate your successes.

A conscious and deliberate discussion must be part of the preliminary planning process. All key players—school board, administration, parents, faculty, and students—should have a voice in the plan. To guide these deliberations, this chapter focuses on three broad goals. First, three different models of intensive scheduling are presented. Second, each of the major variables is operationally defined and examined within the framework of key decision points (questions) for critical analysis (Tables 2–1 through 2–5). The focus questions listed are not intended to be exhaustive. Rather, they represent significant themes that should encourage the formulation of many additional questions. Finally, a systematic process for evaluation of each model with relation to variable analysis is presented, with rubrics for each variable (Tables 2–6 through 2–10).

A systematic process for evaluating extended-block scheduling options can guide you in selecting the approach that will best serve your needs.

Even if your school has already implemented some form of intensive scheduling, the rubrics can serve as instruments for an ongoing evaluation of your efforts. Revisiting these questions may serve to uncover the strengths and weaknesses of the model you have selected. Revisions and refinements should be seen as a healthy and natural process.

COMMON MODELS OF INTENSIVE SCHEDULING

Each of the models included in this section is described in terms of general structural characteristics and specific application variations. Some of the potential advantages and disadvantages are presented solely as points for discussion and example. The specific application of each model should be analyzed within the parameters established by the five significant variables already examined as they apply to each individual school. The examples provided in Figures 2–1 through 2–5 are not meant to be replicated. Rather, they are included as examples for comparison.

The Semester Block

The semester block schedule, also referred to as the 4 × 4, 2 × 4, and semester schedule, is one of the most commonly used forms of intensive scheduling. The 180-day school year is divided into two 90-day semesters, and each school day is divided into four blocks of approximately 90 minutes each. In the Virginia High School Plan, "students earn up to 8 credits per year and 32 over four years of high school" by taking four classes at a time (Edwards, 1995, p. 16). The increased scheduling flexibility gives students twice the opportunities to complete required courses as the traditional four-year 180-day schedule.

The application of the curriculum requirements to the semester block schedule allows for considerable variation. Figures 2–1 and 2–2 illustrate two different applications of the semester block.

Compare this to the traditional schedule, where students take six or seven classes each day, and teachers teach five, six, or seven classes each day. Under the semester block, students have fewer classes, and teachers teach three extended blocks each day. They work with 75 to 90 students each day compared to more than 150 students. Twenty-five percent of the teacher's workday can be devoted to instructional planning under the semester block model.

Several other advantages are associated with this form of intensive scheduling. A freshman who fails a course could repeat the course in the fall and schedule the sophomore group during the spring semester. In this way the semester cycling can provide for remediation opportunities by allowing students to catch up should they fail during any given semester.

Acceleration of the curriculum is another attractive feature of the semester schedule. As implemented in Orange County High in Virginia, a remarkable transformation took place as faculty sought to improve the quality of instruction made possible by intensive scheduling (Figure 2–1).

Initially, increasing the number of credits for graduation seemed the best way to ensure that students used the additional time rather than graduate in three years. More of the same,

FIGURE 2–1   A Four-Year 9–12 Virginia High School Program with AP College-Level Credit Courses (Semester-Length Courses and Four-Period Day)

Grade 9	Grade 10	Grade 11	Grade 12
First 90-Day Session			
English 9	English 10	English 11	AP English Prep.
Earth Science	Algebra II	Language I	AP Lang. Prep.
PE/Health I	Keyboarding	AP U.S. History Prep.	AP Calculus Prep.
Band/Elective	Band/Elective	AP Biology Prep.	Physics
Second 90-Day Session			
World Geography	PE/Health II	Pre-Calculus	AP English
Biology I	Geometry	Language II	AP Language
Algebra I	Chemistry	AP U.S. History	AP Calculus
Band/Elective	Band/Elective	AP Biology	U.S. Government

Source: From "The 4 × 4 Plan" by C. M. Edwards, Jr., *Educational Leadership,* Vol. 55, No. 3, 1995, p. 17. Used with permission.

FIGURE 2–2   **A Four-Year Intensive Block Schedule at General McLane High School**

Grade 9	Grade 10	Grade 11	Grade 12
First Semester			
English	English	English	English
U.S. History	U.S. History	Econ./Government	Arts/Humanities
PE/Health	PE or Driver's Ed.	PE/Health	PE/Health
Electives[a]	Electives[a]	Electives[a]	Electives[a]
Second Semester			
Science	Science	Science	Electives[a]
Mathematics	Mathematics	Mathematics	
PE/Health	PE or Driver's Ed.	PE/Health	
Electives[a]	Electives[a]	Electives[a]	

[a]A number of elective courses are offered with variable credits in Technology, Language, Family Living, Music, and Art.

> *however, even if provided more efficiently, is not a significant improvement. This reality led 4 × 4 advocates to a major breakthrough: with one minor policy change, the education system almost remakes itself. (Edwards, 1995, p. 17)*

Students can compress a two-course sequence into one year and can move through a program at a pace that can allow them earlier access to college-level courses or career training opportunities (Figure 2–3) in commercial schools, apprenticeship programs, with employers, or through online schooling. Students who successfully complete coursework sequences are actually rewarded as they "bank" or reserve time for options during their junior and senior year.

The semester schedule may present some difficulties not encountered by other models. For example, it may be very difficult to provide integrated academic experiences, team planning, and team teaching using teachers from different academic disciplines, since students are not enrolled in all four core courses during the same semester. The availability of certain community resources for field trips or

FIGURE 2–3   **Technical/Vocational Studies: A 21-Credit Diploma (Semester-Length Courses and Four-Period Day)**

Grade 9	Grade 10	Grade 11	Grade 12
First 90-Day Session			
English 9	English 10	English 11	English 12
Earth Science	Informal Geometry	Drafting I	U.S. Government
Algebra Prep.	Biology I	Auto Mechanics	Auto Mechanics
PE/Health I	Design II	(2 credits)	(2 credits)
Second 90-Day Session			
World Geography	PE/Heath II	U.S. History	
Health/Driver's Ed.	Algebra II	Work Experience Class	Full-Time
Algebra I CORD	Auto Mechanics	Auto Mechanics	Work
Design I	(2 credits)	(2 credits)	Experience

Source: From "The 4 × 4 Plan" by C. M. Edwards, Jr., *Educational Leadership*, Vol. 55, No. 3, 1995, p. 18. Used with permission.

field studies in the sciences may be impaired. Standardized tests taken by students during the spring semester may place students at a disadvantage in subjects that were completed in the fall. Also, college prep students may be at a disadvantage in taking the SATs. Guidance counselors need to be vigilant in seeing that college-bound students complete geometry by the end of their sophomore year if they plan to take the SATs in the fall of their junior year. This may require doubling up on math courses during ninth or tenth grade.

Additionally, students who are absent for an extended period of time may have difficulty catching up. It is not unusual for a student to miss two weeks of school because of an illness like mononucleosis, or after surgery. They will have missed the equivalent of a month on a traditional schedule. Finally, retention of skills from one year to the next may be jeopardized if a student completes a pre-requisite course in the fall and enrolls in the next course the following fall, or in the spring of the next academic year.

Alternating Blocks

The alternating-block schedule differs from the semester block in that students rotate through an "A and B daily schedule" during the entire year for core subjects, and through part of the year for elective or noncore subjects. For example, on Monday the students follow the "A schedule," attending two of the academic core subjects and two or more of the noncore subjects. On Tuesday, they are on the "B schedule," meeting with two different teachers for two different core subjects, and attending the same or different noncore classes.

Figure 2–4 illustrates the alternating nature of this form of intensive scheduling where students essentially see their core subject teachers every other school day for the entire year, resulting in 90 days of class meetings of approximately 90 minutes each.

This form of scheduling is the most conservative approach of the models under consideration. Although it departs from the traditional school schedule by allowing for longer time blocks of approximately 90 minutes, it does not allow for the flexibility and creative applications that the semester block, 75-75-30 plan, or parallel block promote. Nor does it effectively reduce a teacher's student load, because one group of 75 to 90 students is arriving every other day. The students are still locked into the pacing of 90 days spread out over the traditional 180-day calendar. Students who fail a course must cycle back through the course again the following year.

FIGURE 2–4   Alternating A/B Block Schedule: Grade 9 Example

Day A	Day B
English 9	Mathematics
Social Studies	Science
PE	Health
Electives[a]	Electives[a]
Tutorial[b]	Tutorial[b]

[a]Electives may include Languages, Art, Music, and Technology.

[b]Tutorial may be provided for enrichment or remediation in core subjects.

FIGURE 2–5   **The 75-75-30 Plan: Grade 10 Example**

First 75-Day Session	Second 75-Day Session	30-Day Session
English 10	Algebra II	English Enrichment
U.S. History	Biology I	Biology Remediation
PE/Health	Driver's Ed.	Art Mini-Elective
Language I	Elective	History Mini-Elective

Another potential disadvantage relates to student absenteeism. Suppose that a student is scheduled to attend his or her math class on Monday but is absent on that day. He or she was not scheduled to attend on the previous Friday and will not be back in the cycle again until Wednesday. In this situation, the teacher has not had classroom contact with the student for six days. Building 45-minute tutorial periods into each school day can help alleviate this problem.

The alternating block does have advantages, however. Consider a school that emphasizes an integrated curriculum, team teaching and planning, and a house concept where teams of teachers move with students through grades 9 to 12. Under these conditions, the regular contact with all core teachers and core subjects throughout the entire academic year may make this model very appealing.

Alterations of the regular school day caused by assemblies, for example, are probably more evenly distributed on the alternating block schedule. Also, access to community resources may be less of a consideration than for the semester block. Finally, because students are enrolled throughout the academic year in all four of their core courses, the performance on standardized tests administered during the spring of the year would not appear to be jeopardized by this form of intensive scheduling.

75-75-30 Plan

This model is similar in design to the semester block but instead uses two 75-day semesters followed by a 30-day session that may be used for remediation or enrichment in any of the core academic subjects, or for student enrollment in a variety of elective courses. It has all of the advantages of the semester block, and allows for 30 days of intensive work as selected by high-performing students. Teachers may assign students who have not developed basic competency in core subjects to academic 30-day blocks for additional instruction and skill development. In schools wishing to offer "mini-elective" courses, this 30-day session can allow for such courses. Figure 2–5 illustrates one application of the 75-75-30 plan.

VARIABLES

Variables that impinge upon the effective use of intensive scheduling do not exist in isolation. Because of the interplay of variables, systemic and extrasystemic, attempting to superimpose one pattern, one model, in every school is fraught with otherwise avoidable complications and probable failure. Thus, this examination of significant variables affords an opportunity to focus on specific areas of inquiry that must be developed thoroughly before any model is adopted for use. Use Tables 2–1 through 2–5 to begin to think about the significance of each critical ques-

TABLE 2–1   Focus Questions: Curriculum

1. To what extent is the intensive scheduling model congruent with course requirements for graduation?
2. Under intensive scheduling, will students be provided with the minimum number of hours of instruction for each credit/course?
3. How will integrated curriculum approaches at each grade level be addressed?
4. How will new students (transfers) be cycled into the curriculum sequence?
5. How will students who fail courses be cycled into the sequence?
6. In what ways can intensive scheduling accommodate acceleration of the curriculum for students?
7. How will students enrolled in vocational schools be accommodated in their "home school" under intensive scheduling?
8. How will teachers be able to allocate adequate time to course "content" in order to complete the course of study as designed?

tion within the structure of your school and community. Compare your analysis with that of others involved in the planning process by completing each of the five evaluation rubrics at the end of the chapter.

Curriculum

The variable that draws the most attention from schools considering intensive scheduling is the scope and sequence of courses required for grade promotion and high school graduation. Any application of an intensive scheduling model must take into account both core (academic) course requirements in mathematics, science, English, and social studies and noncore course requirements in health and physical education, music, art, technology, and foreign language. Local school districts design course requirements that must comply with various state guidelines and must consider federal guidelines, particularly where funding allocations require adherence to entitlement guidelines. Given these state and federal mandates, the school district curriculum takes its own shape, and students are scheduled into both core and noncore courses during each academic year.

Several questions need to be addressed with regard to how school curriculum as a significant variable may impact the design and subsequent effectiveness of intensive scheduling. Eight crucial questions are posed in Table 2–1.

As all of the shareholders participate actively in response to these and other related questions that are certain to surface, the essence of the curriculum itself becomes analyzed under one overarching question: "What is best for our students?" Depending on the model of block scheduling, the answers may differ, and the relative impact of curriculum in the decision-making process may intensify or decrease. For example, under an alternating block plan, it may be easier to allow for integrated experiences between math and science classrooms than would be possible under a semester block scheduling plan in which students do not have math and science during the same semester. The whole consideration of integrated experiences may be irrelevant if school policy and practice do not incorporate formally integrated experiences among the academic disciplines.

Instructional Methods

Schools that have implemented intensive scheduling in one form or another have routinely reported an increased opportunity for the application of teaching techniques that engage students as active learners, encourage application of content and process skills, and promote critical thinking (O'Neil, 1995). Given that impressive potential, other schools also report teacher difficulty and/or resistance in the planning and delivering of lessons that make use of longer blocks of instructional time. If the full potential for constructive change is to be realized through the use of intensive scheduling as a tool, several methodological questions must be answered (Table 2–2).

As with curriculum, candid discussion and exchange of various responses to these questions will necessarily uncover the real approach taken by teachers in the delivery of instruction. Resistance to intensive scheduling may come from a cadre of faculty who are very comfortable with the methods they routinely use because they can provide empirical evidence that it has a favorable impact on student achievement. Still other faculty may defend lecture-recitation not on the basis of empirical evidence but because they feel they will not have the time or do not want to spend the time to develop new lesson and unit plans for courses they have already been teaching for a number of years. On the other hand, those faculty who are already using more student-centered instructional techniques may see the transition to extended time periods as a godsend.

Resistance also may come from school administrators. If it is determined that a departure from traditional didactic approaches requires allocation of capital for technology, for example, administrators may be hard pressed to justify budget adjustments to other shareholders in the school. For principals who view an effective classroom as one where teachers talk and students sit and listen, alternative approaches to instruction may appear as unproductive and disruptive. However, principals who support active learning strategies may encourage the use of student-centered techniques within the extended time blocks.

Students unaccustomed to active classroom climates may actively or passively resist attempts made by teachers to engage them as active learners and move them beyond lower cognitive levels. Under the traditional 45-minute class schedule,

TABLE 2–2 Focus Questions: Instructional Methods

1. What methods of instruction can be better implemented with extended blocks of class time?
2. What teaching methods are already part of the teaching style of the school faculty?
3. How receptive will students be to teaching strategies that require more active student roles?
4. What additional resources will be needed in order to use different instructional methods?
5. What teaching strategies develop higher level cognitive skills in my subject matter discipline?
6. How supportive are building administrators of nontraditional, student-centered teaching methods?
7. What staff development programs must be delivered in order to train faculty in the use of alternative methods of teaching?
8. How much additional planning time will be needed to convert existing lesson plans into plans that utilize different methodology?

they may have been successful serving as receptacles of information. Their parents also may question the motives for changing to intensive scheduling and the infusion of nontraditional methods of instruction. "Students' attitudes toward block scheduling reflect how effective they perceive their teachers to be" (O'Neil, 1995, p. 14).

To develop a proactive position, questions about instructional methods must be raised and debated. The obstacles to change are clearly identified and rationally addressed. By anticipating the problems associated with shifts in teaching practice toward active learning, one can expect a smoother, though not flawless, transition for teachers, students, parents, and administrators.

Resource Allocation

The term *resources* includes human, capital, physical, and community resources as they are individually and collectively accessed by the school. Human resources include faculty, students, administrators, ancillary staff, and community members. Capital resources are the budget allocations affected by intensive scheduling. Physical resources include the physical facility, such as classrooms, laboratories, technology, and the library. Community resources may be considered as off-campus sites used by faculty for various instructional purposes, such as theaters, science field trip locations, and business and industry partnerships. As with the other variables, Table 2–3 offers questions to stimulate dialogue and evaluate each intensive scheduling model to be presented.

Depending on one's perspective, the last question may be of greatest importance. It is in many ways connected to all other issues offered here. An objective assessment of the allocation of all resources dedicated toward the delivery of best possible service should generate a list of student-oriented priorities. Healthy debates will certainly ensue regarding staff and student assignment to core and non-core courses; pros and cons of ability grouping; fairness and equity of access to materials and supplies; and effective use of technology, laboratory space, library holdings, community resources, and personnel. These debates must occur if the shareholders in the school are to form a consensus and take ownership of the model of intensive scheduling that emerges from these deliberations.

TABLE 2–3 Focus Questions: Resource Allocation

1. How will teachers be assigned to course offerings under an intensive scheduling model?
2. What effect will intensive scheduling have on faculty/class size?
3. What changes will be made in grouping policy, heterogeneous or homogeneous?
4. What impact will intensive scheduling have on allocation of faculty for delivery of programs for students with special needs?
5. What impact is anticipated on the demand for classroom, laboratory, and library space and scheduling?
6. What accommodations will be needed for student materials such as textbooks, supplemental materials, audiovisual aids, and computer hardware and software?
7. What community resources will be made more or less available to teachers and students?
8. What are the added costs associated with each model of intensive scheduling?

TABLE 2–4   Focus Questions: Contractual Obligations

1. How is each model of intensive scheduling congruent with contract language on teacher planning/preparation time?
2. Will the implementation of intensive scheduling require additional staff development not addressed in the contract?
3. What is the impact of the teacher seniority accommodations required by each intensive scheduling model?
4. How does this model alter the workday/school year?
5. How will this model affect nonteaching duty assignments during the school day?
6. If additional costs are to be incurred, how will this affect other budget categories?
7. Can additional staff development training be used toward inservice credit allocation for certification, tenure, or salary schedule advancement?
8. How will movement to intensive scheduling influence teacher evaluations conducted by school administrators?

Contractual Obligations

The teacher contract serves as a significant variable affecting any reform or restructuring effort in education. In some school districts the teacher contract exerts a more powerful influence on the potential of any reform agenda. Faculty and school boards are well advised to review the articles of agreement that may promote or thwart changes necessary to move toward the implementation of any intensive scheduling model under study.

In schools where teacher empowerment has been established, participants have already acted in concert with other key players in decision-making processes in real and substantial ways. In these schools, teachers are more comfortable with the challenge of reform and serve as agents of change on a collaborative team. With this type of empowered history, a clearer picture may emerge regarding the role of the contract in proposed reform efforts.

Whether or not the contractual obligations serve as an obstacle to intensive scheduling depends more on the contract than on the model itself. Many standard agreements require that a set number of minutes per day or week be provided for instruction planning and preparation. Few would argue the need for this time. But is it imperative that every teacher be given the same number of minutes each day of each week of each grading period, or is it possible to provide over the course of the school year an equitable time allotment for planning? As each model is examined, scheduling flexibility may surface as a more attractive feature of one model than another. Table 2–4 raises several relevant questions for your consideration.

Assessment

For purposes of this discussion, assessment of student performance as a significant variable refers to nonstandardized and standardized forms of measuring student academic performance. Teacher-made tests, assignments, portfolios, student products, and the like constitute nonstandardized, routinely used formats. Standardized tests selected at either the district or state level represent another commonly used battery of instruments designed to measure something of value about student achievement or aptitude. Responses to several important questions about assessment and intensive scheduling should prove productive.

TABLE 2–5 Focus Questions: Assessment of Student Performance

1. How will teachers adjust their methods of evaluation of student performance?

2. What alternative methods of assessment can be better implemented with intensive scheduling?

3. What impact will intensive scheduling have on student retention?

4. How does each model promote/impair the successful completion of long-range student projects?

5. What effect will longer time blocks have on student attention to instruction and on-task behavior?

6. How does each model address student absenteeism and its relationship to student performance?

7. How will the current school district standardized testing procedure and schedule have to be modified under each model?

8. What impact is anticipated, under each model, on student performance on standardized tests?

The provision of additional time may afford teachers the opportunity to use traditional assessments such as quizzes or practice assignments on a more frequent basis. It may also increase the use of more guided practice exercises prior to the assignment of independent practice or homework. Beyond these commonly used formats, teachers may find that they have more time to incorporate student presentations, debates, hands-on activities, or role-playing exercises and simulations. It is also possible that teachers will simply lecture for twice as long or will give students class time to complete assignments that had traditionally been given as homework. How each teacher uses the extended time frame for nonstandardized student assessment is driven more by the teacher than by the model of intensive scheduling selected.

If a school district's standardized testing policy and schedule is fixed and inflexible, administered only in the spring of the academic year, students enrolled in particular courses only during the fall semester may be at a marked disadvantage with respect to students who are enrolled during the spring semester. The alternating block schedule may not create this disadvantage, but it may create a short-term disadvantage because students are not in contact with the teacher every day through the completion of the course. The variations in intensive scheduling designs implemented by schools across the country may account for variations in the reported impact on student performance on nonstandardized and standardized formats.

When each model is examined with reference to these focus questions (Table 2–5), a logical decision can be reached and obstacles can be anticipated. The focus questions can also serve as a source of major points to be considered for the ongoing evaluation of the effectiveness of intensive scheduling once initiated.

THE RUBRICS

Tables 2–6 through 2–10 are designed to allow you to evaluate and compare the different models of intensive scheduling presented in this chapter. As you consider each question, determine the degree to which each model meets the needs of your school community with regard to curriculum, instructional methods, resource allocation, contractual obligations, and assessment of student performance. Use the five-point continuum to help you in these deliberations, with five (5) indicating an excellent fit and one (1) indicating a poor fit.

Eight questions are listed in each rubric, but other critical questions may be added. Other models of intensive scheduling may be evaluated with the same rubrics. Once the rubrics have been completed by each stakeholder in the process, use these to help guide the decision-making process.

TABLE 2–6   Curriculum: Evaluation Rubric

	Intensive Block Model			
Focus Questions	Semester	Alternating	75-75-30	Other
1. To what extent is the intensive scheduling model congruent with course requirements for graduation?	5 4 3 2 1	5 4 3 2 1	5 4 3 2 1	5 4 3 2 1
2. Under intensive scheduling, will students be provided with the minimum number of hours of instruction for each credit/course?	5 4 3 2 1	5 4 3 2 1	5 4 3 2 1	5 4 3 2 1
3. How will integrated curriculum approaches at each grade level be addressed?	5 4 3 2 1	5 4 3 2 1	5 4 3 2 1	5 4 3 2 1
4. How will new students (transfers) be cycled into the curriculum sequence?	5 4 3 2 1	5 4 3 2 1	5 4 3 2 1	5 4 3 2 1
5. How will students who fail courses be cycled into the sequence?	5 4 3 2 1	5 4 3 2 1	5 4 3 2 1	5 4 3 2 1
6. In what ways can intensive scheduling accommodate acceleration of the curriculum for students?	5 4 3 2 1	5 4 3 2 1	5 4 3 2 1	5 4 3 2 1
7. How will students enrolled in vocational schools be accommodated in their "home school"?	5 4 3 2 1	5 4 3 2 1	5 4 3 2 1	5 4 3 2 1
8. How will teachers be able to allocate adequate time to course "content" in order to complete the course of study as designed?	5 4 3 2 1	5 4 3 2 1	5 4 3 2 1	5 4 3 2 1
Other Questions (List and Rate)				
9.	5 4 3 2 1	5 4 3 2 1	5 4 3 2 1	5 4 3 2 1
10.	5 4 3 2 1	5 4 3 2 1	5 4 3 2 1	5 4 3 2 1
11.	5 4 3 2 1	5 4 3 2 1	5 4 3 2 1	5 4 3 2 1

TABLE 2–7 Instructional Methods: Evaluation Rubric

| | Intensive Block Model | | | |
Focus Questions	Semester	Alternating	75-75-30	Other
1. What methods of instruction can be better implemented with extended blocks of class time?	5 4 3 2 1	5 4 3 2 1	5 4 3 2 1	5 4 3 2 1
2. What teaching methods are already part of the teaching style of the school faculty?	5 4 3 2 1	5 4 3 2 1	5 4 3 2 1	5 4 3 2 1
3. How receptive will students be to teaching strategies that require more active student roles?	5 4 3 2 1	5 4 3 2 1	5 4 3 2 1	5 4 3 2 1
4. What additional resources will be needed in order to use different instructional methods?	5 4 3 2 1	5 4 3 2 1	5 4 3 2 1	5 4 3 2 1
5. What teaching strategies develop higher level cognitive skills in my subject-matter discipline?	5 4 3 2 1	5 4 3 2 1	5 4 3 2 1	5 4 3 2 1
6. How supportive are building administrators of nontraditional, student-centered teaching methods?	5 4 3 2 1	5 4 3 2 1	5 4 3 2 1	5 4 3 2 1
7. What staff development programs must be delivered in order to train faculty in the use of alternative methods of teaching?	5 4 3 2 1	5 4 3 2 1	5 4 3 2 1	5 4 3 2 1
8. How much additional planning time will be needed to convert existing lesson plans into plans that use different methodology?	5 4 3 2 1	5 4 3 2 1	5 4 3 2 1	5 4 3 2 1
Other Questions (List and Rate)				
9.	5 4 3 2 1	5 4 3 2 1	5 4 3 2 1	5 4 3 2 1
10.	5 4 3 2 1	5 4 3 2 1	5 4 3 2 1	5 4 3 2 1
11.	5 4 3 2 1	5 4 3 2 1	5 4 3 2 1	5 4 3 2 1

TABLE 2–8 Resource Allocation: Evaluation Rubric

Focus Questions	Intensive Block Model			
	Semester	Alternating	75-75-30	Other
1. How will teachers be assigned to course offerings under an intensive scheduling model?	5 4 3 2 1	5 4 3 2 1	5 4 3 2 1	5 4 3 2 1
2. What effect will intensive scheduling have on faculty/class size?	5 4 3 2 1	5 4 3 2 1	5 4 3 2 1	5 4 3 2 1
3. What changes will be made in grouping policy, heterogeneous or homogeneous?	5 4 3 2 1	5 4 3 2 1	5 4 3 2 1	5 4 3 2 1
4. What impact will intensive scheduling have on allocation of faculty for delivery of programs for students with special needs?	5 4 3 2 1	5 4 3 2 1	5 4 3 2 1	5 4 3 2 1
5. What impact is anticipated on the demand for classroom, laboratory, and library space and scheduling?	5 4 3 2 1	5 4 3 2 1	5 4 3 2 1	5 4 3 2 1
6. What accommodations will be needed for student materials such as textbooks, supplemental materials, audiovisual aids, computer hardware and software, etc.?	5 4 3 2 1	5 4 3 2 1	5 4 3 2 1	5 4 3 2 1
7. What community resources will be made more or less available to teachers and students?	5 4 3 2 1	5 4 3 2 1	5 4 3 2 1	5 4 3 2 1
8. What are the added costs associated with each model of intensive scheduling?	5 4 3 2 1	5 4 3 2 1	5 4 3 2 1	5 4 3 2 1
Other Questions (List and Rate)				
9.	5 4 3 2 1	5 4 3 2 1	5 4 3 2 1	5 4 3 2 1
10.	5 4 3 2 1	5 4 3 2 1	5 4 3 2 1	5 4 3 2 1
11.	5 4 3 2 1	5 4 3 2 1	5 4 3 2 1	5 4 3 2 1

TABLE 2–9   Contractual Obligations: Evaluation Rubric

Focus Questions	Intensive Block Model			
	Semester	Alternating	75-75-30	Other
1. How is each model of intensive scheduling congruent with contract language on teacher planning/preparation time?	5 4 3 2 1	5 4 3 2 1	5 4 3 2 1	5 4 3 2 1
2. Will the implementation of intensive scheduling require additional staff development not addressed in the contract?	5 4 3 2 1	5 4 3 2 1	5 4 3 2 1	5 4 3 2 1
3. How does teacher seniority impact accommodations required by each intensive scheduling model?	5 4 3 2 1	5 4 3 2 1	5 4 3 2 1	5 4 3 2 1
4. How does this model alter the workday/school year?	5 4 3 2 1	5 4 3 2 1	5 4 3 2 1	5 4 3 2 1
5. How will this model influence nonteaching duty assignments during the school day?	5 4 3 2 1	5 4 3 2 1	5 4 3 2 1	5 4 3 2 1
6. If additional costs are to be incurred, how will this affect other budget categories?	5 4 3 2 1	5 4 3 2 1	5 4 3 2 1	5 4 3 2 1
7. Can additional staff development training be used toward inservice credit allocation for certification, tenure, and salary schedule advancement?	5 4 3 2 1	5 4 3 2 1	5 4 3 2 1	5 4 3 2 1
8. How will movement to intensive scheduling affect teacher evaluations conducted by school administrators?	5 4 3 2 1	5 4 3 2 1	5 4 3 2 1	5 4 3 2 1
Other Questions (List and Rate)				
9.	5 4 3 2 1	5 4 3 2 1	5 4 3 2 1	5 4 3 2 1
10.	5 4 3 2 1	5 4 3 2 1	5 4 3 2 1	5 4 3 2 1
11.	5 4 3 2 1	5 4 3 2 1	5 4 3 2 1	5 4 3 2 1

TABLE 2–10   Assessment: Evaluation Rubric

| Focus Questions | Intensive Block Model | | | |
	Semester	Alternating	75-75-30	Other
1. How will teachers adjust their methods of evaluation of student performance?	5 4 3 2 1	5 4 3 2 1	5 4 3 2 1	5 4 3 2 1
2. What alternative methods of assessment can be better implemented with intensive scheduling?	5 4 3 2 1	5 4 3 2 1	5 4 3 2 1	5 4 3 2 1
3. What impact will intensive scheduling have on student retention?	5 4 3 2 1	5 4 3 2 1	5 4 3 2 1	5 4 3 2 1
4. How does each model promote/impair the successful completion of long-range student projects?	5 4 3 2 1	5 4 3 2 1	5 4 3 2 1	5 4 3 2 1
5. What effect will longer time blocks have on student attention to instruction and on-task behavior?	5 4 3 2 1	5 4 3 2 1	5 4 3 2 1	5 4 3 2 1
6. How does each model address student absenteeism and its relationship to student performance?	5 4 3 2 1	5 4 3 2 1	5 4 3 2 1	5 4 3 2 1
7. How will the school district's current standardized testing procedure/schedule have to be modified under each model?	5 4 3 2 1	5 4 3 2 1	5 4 3 2 1	5 4 3 2 1
8. What impact is anticipated, under each model, on student performance on standardized tests?	5 4 3 2 1	5 4 3 2 1	5 4 3 2 1	5 4 3 2 1

Other Questions (List and Rate)

	Semester	Alternating	75-75-30	Other
9.	5 4 3 2 1	5 4 3 2 1	5 4 3 2 1	5 4 3 2 1
10.	5 4 3 2 1	5 4 3 2 1	5 4 3 2 1	5 4 3 2 1
11.	5 4 3 2 1	5 4 3 2 1	5 4 3 2 1	5 4 3 2 1

■ 3
Cooperative and Collaborative Strategies

AESOP TOLD A story of a man who had four sons. This man loved his sons very much, but they worried him a great deal because they were always fighting with each other. The father tried but was unable to stop their arguing.

The father asked himself, "What can I do to show my sons it is wrong to act this way?" One morning the man showed his sons a bundle of sticks. He asked them, "Which one of you can break this bundle of sticks?"

Each of the sons tried but not one of them could do it. The father then unwrapped the bundle and gave each of his sons a single stick. "Now, which of you can break the sticks?"

Each of them could easily do so. "My sons," the father said, "each of you alone is weak. He is as easy to injure as one of these sticks. But if you will stick together, you will be as strong as the bundle of sticks."

Applying the concept of cooperation to the classroom is as easy as what the father did with his sons: bundle your students together into a safe, productive, strong unit. As the extended-block period allows for students to spend longer periods of time together, the opportunities to use cooperative strategies increase. With a small amount of background knowledge and adherence to several guiding principles, you will find cooperative learning a very effective instructional technique to enhance what you are doing in the extended-block period.

BACKGROUND

Interest in the theories of cooperation and studies of these theories have been reflected in social psychological research conducted since the late 1800s. The research on specific application of these theories to school-age children and classroom learning situations, however, has resulted in a focus on their potential roles in education.

Johnson and Johnson began using learning groups in classroom situations in the 1960s. They investigated inquiry learning using cooperative groups at the elementary level and cooperative structures with adolescents to refocus student attention and subsequent behaviors toward academic goals (Johnson & Johnson, 1989). Research into cooperative group structures encouraged the Johnsons and others to refine the use of cooperative learning in education.

Many theorists tested and modified the conclusions relevant to the effects of cooperation on human, and specifically, student learning (Johnson & Johnson, 1991; Shara, Ackerman, & Hertz-Lazarowitz, 1979; Slavin, 1987). Seta, Paulus, and Schkade (1976) investigated the use of cooperative instruction on group performance. They found that small groups given cooperative instructions performed complex tasks better than groups that were given competitive instructions. When attempting to produce high achievement, researchers have discovered that cooperative efforts are consistently superior to competitive and individualistic efforts (Johnson & Johnson, 1989).

A meta-analysis of research strongly supports classroom approaches to instruction that encourage students to work cooperatively. Toepfer (1990) concluded that cooperative learning activities develop a sense of positive interdependence as students work together and become responsible for each other. Cooperative strategies facilitate effective use of block scheduling.

COOPERATIVE LEARNING IS NOT JUST ANOTHER NAME FOR GROUP WORK

Through the development of cooperative structures, we can identify dimensions inherent in cooperative learning techniques that have proved necessary to promote positive cognitive and affective outcomes for participating learners. There are many specific cooperative learning methods, which vary in a variety of ways, but they are united in the application of basic principles of heterogeneity of groups, positive group interdependence, face-to-face promotive interaction, individual accountability, and interpersonal social skills development.

Teacher dependency in cooperative structures is minimized as students assume greater responsibility for their learning by being accountable to themselves and their peers. Cooperation as an instructional strategy "shifts the responsibility of learning from the teacher to the students" (Behounek, Rosenbaum, Brown, & Burcalow, 1988, p. 13).

The heterogeneous nature of cooperative learning groups allows for maximization of student contributions. When the teacher thoughtfully orchestrates the composition of groups within the classroom, members of the groups benefit from multiple contributions and diverse perspectives. Teachers and students then view diversity as a strength that promotes greater depth and breadth of learning. Daily involvement with individuals who are different also increases acceptance of those individual differences by promoting tolerance and appreciation of others' contributions.

Cooperative learning replaces reliance on the teacher with interdependence among group members. Teachers structure class activities in such a way that each group member's contribution is necessary for successful completion of the assigned task. Students thus "develop the feeling that they are responsible for and accountable to the group (as well as to themselves) for doing their best" (Strother, 1990, p. 158). Dependence on one's group members and recognized dependence of others on oneself improves attitudes toward peers as supporters and toward oneself through higher self-esteem. Within a cooperative group, students realize that whatever they do to help their peers learn the material benefits them as well. The results are that students care about each other and provide help to their classmates when it is needed. This positive group interdependency is a crucial factor in understanding and successfully implementing cooperative techniques in the classroom.

As group members encourage and facilitate each others' efforts to achieve, they assist and help each other, exchange resources, give each other feedback, disagree and argue, advocate increased effort to achieve mutual goals, influence and trust each other, and demonstrate the motivation for mutual benefit (Johnson & Johnson, 1989, p. 76).

During promotive face-to-face interaction, students are given opportunities to share knowledge and information orally. Within the small groups, individuals discuss the material under study and encourage and support their group members' efforts to achieve. This oral exchange benefits the speaker because of the cognitive processing required to explain, elaborate, and summarize information. The listener also benefits from the opportunity to learn and incorporate knowledge and reasoning from another perspective. These opportunities provide for learning through multiple sensory channels, thus promoting greater understanding, critical thinking skills, and long-term retention of material studied. This promotion of physically close communication provides students with a chance to learn how to read body language and the subtle nuances of language. Students develop the ability to work with others and learn to use strengths that their peers have when given opportunities to interact with each other. Promotive face-to-face interaction is an important principle of cooperative learning strategies.

Individual accountability refers to the "conviction in the groups that each group member needs to know the material and explain it rationally" (Johnson & Johnson, 1989, p. 180). In cooperative group structures, each student perceives that he or she is individually responsible for completing the given task. This ensures that no one member of the group will allow others to do the majority of the given assignment, because every person within the group is required to prove mastery of the material under investigation. Mastery can be proved through a written assignment or an oral task. The only way the group can be successful is if every individual member of the group has learned. Each group member is constantly challenged to contribute a fair share, to prove his or her own worth to the group and to him- or herself. This individual accountability for learning increases individual achievement, particularly in weak skill areas.

To reinforce individual accountability, each student's mastery of the material is assessed. Although group members practice together, individuals are tested to monitor their independent skill attainment. Group success depends on the individual learning of each of the group's members; therefore, the group's task is to prepare its members to succeed on individual assessments.

As secondary teachers, we readily admit that our adolescent students do not have well-developed interpersonal skills. Emotional bickering, personal attacks, misplaced anger, and inability to forgive often prevent students from getting along with an extended peer group as well as with authority figures. Without assistance to develop beyond these interpersonal obstacles, students will find adult life frustrating at the very least. Cooperative learning provides a natural avenue for addressing this development.

Placement in a small, heterogeneous group of peers allows students many opportunities to practice and refine fundamental social skills that assist individual growth in listening, sharing, responsibility, and tolerance. Such simple tasks as moving into groups quickly and quietly, bringing appropriate materials to the group, listening when other group members speak, and taking turns with materials needed in the group all give adolescents the chance to develop their own social skills, in a way that has a positive impact on others around them. These basic skills then can evolve into higher order skills, such as encouraging others, redirecting self and others, accepting and delivering gentle, constructive criticism, and being patient with those who disagree or who have not developed those fundamental interpersonal skills.

Effective cooperative learning addresses academic and social goals.

MAKING COOPERATIVE LEARNING WORK

A colleague recalls her memories of group work from a high school English class: "I was put into a group with four of my peers and told to work together to create a poem about compromise. I don't remember much about the poem itself. What I do remember is the two girls in my group who wrote the poem while I talked with the two basketball players in my group about the upcoming ball game. I also remember all of us receiving an A for the poem and having it hung on the classroom wall for parent night . . . with all five signatures as authors."

In considering the characteristics common to successful cooperative learning structures, the teacher must ask, "How can I be sure all of these are operating in my classroom?" Luckily, the answer is simpler than many people realize and easier to do than you may suspect. When each of these characteristics is considered relative to the classroom as a whole, they can be provided for and monitored. And because the extended-block schedule provides longer periods of time in which to implement cooperative strategies, students are involved throughout the class meeting.

When considering the formation of smaller groups in your classroom, first look at the composition of the whole group. Determine the similarities and differences that operate to enhance and prohibit progress during your class meetings. Identify strengths and weaknesses of each student as well as those of the class as a whole. In this way you can build on those characteristics to maximize individual and group performance.

A wide variety of characteristics can be used to develop effective cooperative groups. These can include physical, social, academic, and emotional attributes.

- *Physical characteristics* are traits that are readily observable about the person's body features. These are often the means by which people get a first impression of others.
- *Social skills* are those qualities that enable a person to get along with others. They are seen as students deal with their peers and teachers both informally and in structured situations.
- *Academic attributes* are those skills that reflect the subject-area knowledge of the learner. These skills are directly related to the specific academic subject for which the cooperative learning task is being planned, and the skills that should be considered change with the subject of study.
- *Emotional characteristics* are those that address feelings of individual students. As secondary teachers are well aware, these often are unstable in adolescents, shifting quickly and unpredictably during the course of any one school term.

In planning cooperative learning groups, the teacher must focus on those characteristics that are typical of each given student and that predominate in their daily behavior. Table 3–1 provides a summary of the specific characteristics that should be considered when developing any heterogeneous group for a cooperative learning situation.

The size of the heterogeneous groups that you are using depends on your level of comfort with the activity, content, and students, the number of students assigned to your classroom, and the specific cooperative learning structure you are using. Many teachers prefer smaller groups even if it means a greater number of groups to monitor in any given class period. It seems that groups larger than four limit students' progress, facilitate individual students' tendency to avoid participating, and leave teachers feeling frustrated by the difficulty of monitoring group members. On the other hand, pairs are not always appropriate for a given task. Because the extended-block schedule will see these students together for longer periods at a time, in the course of a single class meeting the teacher can facilitate the team building that usually must occur over several days.

Teachers might be best guided to first determine goals for the students in the class, then consider what job responsibilities will exist for group members. Once you have determined the necessary jobs for the task, you can more readily determine the size of the groups, ensuring that each group member has one job at all times. At the conclusion of the section in this chapter on types of cooperative learning structures, Table 3–8 indicates the appropriate size for groups formed for each structure.

TABLE 3–1   Characteristics for Heterogeneous Grouping

- *Physical:* Age, gender, race, height, weight, physical prowess
- *Social:* Leadership, trust, honesty, communication, acceptance, conflict management, perspective taking
- *Academic:* These are subject-specific but include the fundamental skills expected of students in a particular academic area. For example, in a lower level mathematics classroom one might examine students' abilities to add, subtract, divide, multiply, and solve simple equations.
- *Emotional:* Confidence, self-esteem, general happiness, independence, stress

Adolescents seem to find it fairly easy and quite acceptable to connect themselves with a selected peer group and disregard everyone else. Past parental concern with teenage cliques has grown into societal fear of violent adolescent gangs. These groups are successful in their activities, even their illegal activities, because of their cohesiveness, their ability to make members of the group feel a sense of belonging, a sense that the group depends on each individual's very existence and participation. This need to belong can be used effectively in an extremely positive way through the development of positive group interdependence in cooperative group structures. This interdependence can be facilitated by the individual longer periods of time in which students will be interacting under an extended-block schedule.

Positive group interdependence is the product of individual group members sharing a common goal whereby every member of the group gets ahead or fails based on the overall performance of the group members. Individual members of the group realize the job will not get done unless all do their parts. When all group members contribute to the group's activities and thus progress, a sense of collegiality and belonging develops.

Teachers can provide for the development of positive group interdependence by structuring tasks so that one member cannot succeed unless others in their group also succeed. Individual members must realize they can achieve their goals only if other individuals in their group achieve their own goals as well. Individuals can reach the goal only if their peers reach the same goal. For example, each individual in a group may be required to provide biographical information about one specific scientist to their group. Once that information is provided, those individuals have met their own goals. To complete the cooperative learning task, however, the group may be given the task of ranking the contributions of these scientists and defending their rankings with factual information gained about them. Unless all individual group members have contributed, the second goal is unattainable. In this way, individuals work toward personal goals, provided through job assignments and division of responsibilities, and toward group goals, provided through content mastery expectations. Teachers can also structure rewards for established goals that can be realized only when successful performance occurs by each and every individual group member. Frequent opportunities arise for rewards to be given as students remain with teachers for longer periods of time because teachers can more readily recognize positive performance and students can receive individual interaction with their teacher each day under an extended-block schedule.

When considering how to encourage members of each individual group to develop a sense of cohesiveness and camaraderie, one of the first things to do is move the furniture. Tables can be aligned to form tight rectangular arrangements, individual desks can be moved into closed circular formations, and separate chairs can be grouped so students can sit in a round-table formation. These arrangements quickly help stimulate conversation while helping you maintain appropriate noise levels. Students can easily share materials necessary to the task at hand by reaching across the group members to give and receive supplies. Monitoring of participants is facilitated as the teacher can readily see each tightly arranged group as a unit separate from the whole of the classroom. In this way, a teacher can quickly change focus from the whole class to individual groups, and back to individual group members, keeping teacher awareness of progress and problems at a maximum. The teacher's opportunities to engage in direct conversation and instruction with individual groups is also easier because of the physical boundary of each group. *Face to face* and *knee to knee* are phrases to help encourage students to sit closely and work together.

FIGURE 3–1   Furniture Arrangements to Promote Cooperative Learning

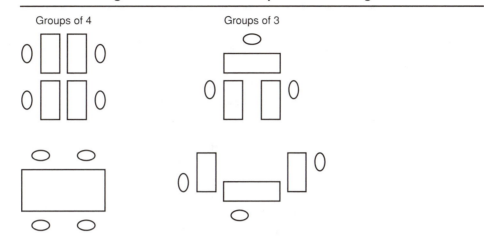

Groups of 4   Groups of 3

This structural reconfiguring of your classroom is very important to the success of any cooperative learning structure you employ. Without the physical closeness of their peers, students will not be able to develop the positive interdependence needed to be successful with their groups. This physical proximity promotes a positive social and motivational situation that can maximize student output. Figure 3–1 shows possible furniture arrangements to promote effective cooperative behaviors.

Individual accountability dictates that all members of the group are responsible for contributing to the group product and for learning the materials assigned. Each member of each group must prove individual mastery of the material studied within the group. Teachers must hold individual students accountable for the work assigned. This accountability occurs during the learning process as well as at the conclusion of the program. During the process, teachers look at what is being accomplished by the group during each step, and who is contributing to the group's progress. Because more progress can be made each day with more time allowed, students readily see their performance and teachers more easily monitor it.

Assignment of specific jobs for each member of each cooperative group makes the teacher's job easier here, as you can then watch for the completion of each subtask as groups work. For example, when one member of each group is assigned the task of recorder, the teacher needs only to walk among the groups and observe who is recording the information and what information is being recorded. This then begins the assessment of individual and group progress, while identifying the level of accountability each individual is meeting. Again, because students in the longer classroom period will spend more time performing their assigned job, they more quickly become adept at doing so. When they are again given that responsibility later in the course, there is little need for reteaching the job role. Table 3–2 provides a brief listing of jobs frequently assigned during cooperative learning structures.

Also important to holding individuals accountable for the work completed are final assessments of the learning that has occurred. At the conclusion of any cooperative learning activity, the teacher must have ready an assessment tool that allows individual students to demonstrate on their own what they have learned. This accountability can be easily built into any cooperative learning structure used. Various structures provide for different ways to address individual accountability, but there are traditional methods that teachers use every day that work well. The assessment is frequently an individual quiz or written test, but can take other

TABLE 3–2   **Job Assignments**

Recorder	Timer	Evaluator
Proofreader	Speaker	Mediator
Researcher	Checker	Teacher contact
Observer	Monitor	Editor
Leader	Reporter	

forms as well. Final written reports, individual oral presentations, individual projects, the completion of a rubric for self-evaluation, and other task-appropriate products can be developed and submitted by students, allowing the teacher to determine individual content mastery.

Cooperative learning activities provide opportunity which students in traditionally structured classrooms do not often have: that of frequent in-depth contacts with their peers. "Cooperative learning is an ideal solution to the problem of providing students . . . with opportunities for nonsuperficial, cooperative interactions" (Slavin, 1995, p. 51). Teachers find, often to their surprise, that students who work in cooperative group structures develop those social skills that enable them both to learn in school and to be more successful in life beyond the school walls. These social skills can be provided for in a variety of ways. Allowing students in cooperative groups an amount of group autonomy gives them time to practice effective social skills. Because the groups are heterogeneous, the composition of each group will color the process that each uses to complete the assigned task. The groups, therefore, need to be allowed to make choices about how to proceed. These choices, however, are always couched in the group's accountability for success and/or failure. Students can monitor their own progress while being frequently observed by the teacher, and can make decisions about who should fulfill specific roles, what materials will be needed, when specific tasks will be completed, and how the final product will look. When students can see progress toward their task completion over one class meeting, they can see the impact of positive participation within the group. Table 3–3 indicates some of the interpersonal skills that secondary students need to focus on during their cooperative group work.

It's worth noting that, although the development of these skills can be surprising to teachers, planning for their development is crucial. Students can learn these skills when they are identified and defined by the teacher; clarified by their peers; modeled by their teacher and their peers; reviewed by the teacher, their peers, and themselves; and revisited frequently. Just as cooperative learning in the extended block allows increased time for and efficient use of the time spent on academic concerns, this large block of time provides wonderful opportunities for social skills vitally important to success well beyond adolescence and the institution of school.

TABLE 3–3   **Interpersonal Skills Development**

Contributing	Sharing
Supporting	Encouraging
Using humor	Listening
Praising	Self-monitoring
Self-preparedness	Taking turns
Asking for help	Criticizing ideas, not people
	Reaching consensus

LOW-RISK COOPERATIVE STRATEGIES

Cooperative strategies are simple, short-term activities that secondary teachers will find invaluable for making efficient use of the time allotted in an extended period. Strategies such as Focus Friends, Talking Tiles, Two-Minute Interviews, Pairs Practice, and Homework Helpers can be used at many points in a lesson during the extended period to increase student involvement with the content material, and involve minimal preparation on the part of the teacher and the students. Cooperative strategies are effective complements to other instructional techniques used within the longer blocks of time in extended periods.

Focus Friends

Those familiar with the K-W-L technique (see Chapter 5) will find the Focus Friends task very similar. Prior to showing a video, giving a lecture, or reading material to students, the teacher divides students into groups of three. Each group is given an index card and told to summarize what they already know about the subject on one side of the card. On the other side of the card, they are told to generate at least three questions (one from each student) about the subject to be examined. The teacher then proceeds with the content presentation. Afterward, the groups of three reconvene and answer the questions that they had initially written. The teacher then brings the class back together as a whole to discuss the new information, clarify questions still held by students, and provide general whole-group reflection of the topic.

Talking Tiles

Talking Tiles uses index cards with the words "Time to Talk" written on them. Teachers can use this technique by placing students in groups of 4 or 5. Students are given an issue to discuss that requires them to offer an opinion or "take a side," with one student speaking at a time—the student holding the Talking Tile. One student is handed the Talking Tile to begin the discussion. The student with the Tile is the only one permitted to talk; all others must listen. The teacher monitors the time, allowing a predetermined amount of time before calling for the Talking Tile to be passed. The Talking Tile is passed to the right, and the receiver of the Tile speaks next. In this way only one person in each group speaks at a time, while all other group members listen and, if the teacher requires, take notes on what others have to contribute.

Two-Minute Interviews

Working with partners can be a time-efficient way for all students in the class to participate. Two-Minute Interviews can be used to involve students in a review of assigned reading done previously in class. The teacher pairs students and gives each pair a sheet of paper. Students each have two minutes to interview their partner about what they remember from the reading. The teacher can then call on students to report on their partners' information and can use this to conduct a review and prepare the class for the day's lesson.

Drill Partners

Drill Partners is a strategy that is most effective as a short-time task, often used immediately before a test or to close a lesson. Students sit with a partner and orally quiz each other on the facts they need to know for a teacher-determined amount of time.

Homework Help

Before reviewing homework assignments as a whole class or collecting them to be graded, Homework Help can be used. Students sit in groups of 2 or 3 and compare answers to their homework. They discuss any for which they do not have the same responses, correct their work when needed, and add the reason they changed those answers. The teacher can then collect the papers or use them for discussion.

COOPERATIVE STRUCTURES TO USE IN THE EXTENDED BLOCK

Reconsideration of cooperative learning structures and their potential for application to classroom instruction has manifested itself in the development of practical programs of cooperation to be used in the school environment. These structures focus on the development of leadership qualities by allowing students to learn to give instructions and play directing roles within group activities. They focus on communication by providing multiple opportunities for students to share ideas and information during the learning process. They focus on trust building as students work with others to promote their own and others' success. Finally, these structures promote cooperation as the umbrella under which students solve problems as they share divergent perspectives to develop convergent responses and ultimately mastery of content material.

Cooperative learning generally refers to preplanned instructional techniques for interaction among students. Various cooperative learning strategies have been developed and applied in classroom settings to enhance the cognitive and affective development of learners. Four commonly used structures are presented here to help secondary teachers implement cooperative learning in the extended-block schedule. These structures were chosen because they have proved effective for secondary content and students, they work efficiently within longer blocks of instructional time, they are fairly simple to implement, and they can be applied in a variety of content areas. The structures can be used independent of other instructional techniques but are also effective when incorporated within extended-block periods as complements to traditional techniques.

Jigsaw

Jigsaw is a cooperative learning method originally developed by Elliott Aronson and his colleagues (Aronson et al., 1978). This method includes task specialization in a cooperative incentive structure. Students are assigned to teams to work on content material that has been divided into sections. Each team member reads different information contained in various sections of given printed material, then meets with members of different teams who have studied the same sections for discussion. Students then return to their original teams and take turns teaching teammates about the section they have studied. Next, individual students take a quiz covering all sections of the material. In Jigsaw, quiz scores contribute only to individual grades (Cooper, 1990; Slavin, 1987).

Jigsaw is a technique that secondary teachers often find useful when students are first introduced to a large amount of new material, although it is also appropriate for reviewing information recently studied. It usually requires independent reading and summation and/or note-taking skills on the part of students. The Jigsaw structure fits especially well into an extended-block schedule because of the time available to integrate the Jigsaw activity itself with teacher introduction and direction initially, teacher redirection and clarification during, and teacher reflection and summation finally. This allows for frequent student checks and tight teacher control in a structured student-active task. Table 3–4 shows how Jigsaw might be used in a 90-minute period.

Think-Pair-Share

Particularly useful in areas of concept development, Think-Pair-Share is a cooperative structure that was developed by Frank Lyman (Lyman, 1981). In this approach, the teacher first presents information to the class as a whole while students are seated in pairs within the larger group. Following the content presentation, the teacher asks questions to the class. Students are then directed to think first of their response for a predetermined amount of time (approximately 15–30 seconds). When the thinking time ends, students are told to discuss their responses with their partner to reach agreement on an answer. When consensus is reached, partners can be called on by the teacher to share their answers with the rest of the class.

Think-Pair-Share works well in the extended-block time period because it allows the teacher and students the opportunity to reconsider material just presented. When incorporated with traditionally difficult content, it provides time for

TABLE 3–4   Application of Jigsaw as a 90-Minute Period

15 minutes	Teacher introduces topic, overviews main points. Teacher identifies topic components, sets goals.
10 minutes	Teacher assigns students to Home Team and Expert Groups. Students physically move into Home Teams. Home Teams clarify individual responsibilities and group goal.
20 minutes	Students physically move into Expert Groups. Expert Groups explore and discuss materials.
15 minutes	Teacher addresses whole class to review goals. Expert Groups match information prepared with identified goals.
20 minutes	Expert Groups return to Home Teams and report.
10 minutes	Teacher addresses whole class for reflection and summation. Individual performance (test, quiz) is usually conducted at a later date, but can be worked into the same class period.

critical consideration of newly learned information and review of essential content. This provides the teacher with immediate feedback on student learning as the learning occurs, which can help teachers make critical instructional decisions: to proceed or to back up for review and clarification. Think-Pair-Share adds variety to a block of difficult new information while refreshing and refocusing the students. It also reinforces information. Think-Pair-Share as a cooperative learning technique can be easily extended to include a writing component. During the first step, "Think," have students write what they think. During the second step, "Pair," they can read what they've written to their partner. Table 3–5 shows the application of Think-Pair-Share in a 90-minute period.

Roundrobin

The Roundrobin structure is very popular with secondary teachers who encourage students to examine the separate components of specific content material. Students using this approach are seated closely together in groups of 4 or 5, with one piece of paper and one writing instrument among them. The teacher asks a question that may have more than one answer (e.g., listing phyla in biology), poses a problem that requires a response with several parts (e.g., listing the progressive steps of a trigonometry problem), or presents an issue that can have many interpretations ("Why might the main character have betrayed his family?"). Students make a list on a single piece of paper by moving the paper around their group. Each group member writes one part of the response, then passes the paper to the person next to them. The paper keeps moving around the group until the teacher calls that time is up or the answer is complete.

Roundrobin is so easy to use it can be an especially efficient technique for the extended-block period. Teachers may use this structure at the beginning of the class meeting to review material previously explored, during the class to check students' learning progress, or as a final review of material explored in that class period. Information written by students can then be discussed immediately or collected by the teacher for evaluation. Table 3–6 shows the use of Roundrobin in a 90-minute period.

Numbered Heads Together

Numbered Heads Together is a cooperative structure that was developed by a classroom teacher in response to the lack of student participation he received when he used the traditional technique whereby he asked a question, too few students volunteered to respond, he called on one of the volunteers, and other students disengaged (Slavin, 1986). By grouping students and structuring the question/an-

TABLE 3–5   Application of Think-Pair-Share within a 90-Minute Period

20 minutes	Teacher assigns students to partners.
	Teacher presents new material.
5–15 minutes	Teacher asks questions.
	Students consider, discuss, share.

TABLE 3–6   Application of Roundrobin within a 90-Minute Period

5 minutes	Teacher forms groups of students, provides materials. Teacher asks the question or poses the problem.
10 minutes	Students respond in writing.
20 minutes	Teacher presents content material.
OR	
20 minutes	Teacher presents content material.
5 minutes	Teacher forms groups of students, provides materials. Teacher asks the question or poses the problem.
10 minutes	Students respond in writing.

swer period so that all students engage in discussion about the issues presented, every student benefits from participation.

To institute Numbered Heads Together, the teacher arranges students in groups of 3 or 4, giving each student within each group an identifying number (1–4). The teacher asks a question of the entire class. Students are then directed to "put your heads together" to discuss the answer and to be sure everyone in their group knows the correct answer.

The teacher then calls a number, and students with that number can raise their hands to respond. If an incorrect answer is given, the teacher can call on others for the correct answer. At any time in the activity, the teacher can interject to clarify information that may be difficult for students. Every student has the opportunity to hear the question, consider a response, listen to others' responses, reconsider his or her response, contribute an answer, and hear the correct answer. Students throughout the class know that anyone can be called on to give an answer. Because of the numbering system, the chances of any individual being called is greater than through volunteering. Students with the correct answer are eager to share because they want their group to be correct, and students without the correct answer want to know it because they don't want to be wrong in front of their peers or let their group down. Thus the lower performers listen and learn, and the higher performers review and teach. Numbered Heads Together is a time-efficient and motivational technique to use in a longer class period because it provides high levels of student involvement while maintaining attention to content. It can be used to begin a class when the topic has been previously explored and the teacher wants to review quickly, during a class period to help students make a transition from one piece of content material to the next, and as a concluding activity to provide summation of important information discussed. Table 3–7 shows the application of Numbered Heads Together in a 90-minute period. Table 3–8 summarizes the various techniques described in this chapter.

TABLE 3–7   Application of Numbered Heads Together in a 90-Minute Period

10 minutes	Teacher reintroduces topic, reviews main points. Teacher assigns groups and numbers individuals within groups. Students move into groups.
10-20 minutes	Teacher asks questions and students respond. During this time teacher clarifies and redirects when needed.

TABLE 3–8   Structures and Significant Components

	Group	Content	Individual
Structure	Size	Application	Accountability[a]
Jigsaw (E. Aronson)	3–4	Introduction, Review	Team Report, Exam
Think-Pair-Share (F. Lyman)	2	Reasoning, Review	Response Sheet, Exam
Roundrobin (S. Kagan)	4–5	Critical Thinking Skills, Practice, Recall	Response Sheet, Exam
Numbered Heads Together (S. Kagan)	3–4	Review, Skills Practice	Oral Responses, Exam

[a]Individual accountability is addressed through two components, that which occurs during and that which occurs following the cooperative learning task.

SUMMARY

Teachers have long been concerned about the time pressures on them in a single school day and throughout the school year. The extended-block schedule finally gives teachers the extended period of time they need to teach essential content to secondary students effectively. The longer block of time may not be used to its best advantage, however, with only traditional teaching techniques. Integrating cooperative learning strategies with traditional instructional techniques will help teachers make efficient use of that time. Increased student participation, improved academic achievement, and students who cooperate—that is the formula for success.

■ 4
A Time for Inquiry and Discovery

TWO MODELS OF instruction that are well suited for use in the extended block are inquiry and learning cycle. Each model has a syntax that allows students to learn as active participants at critical points in each lesson. Active learning strategies such as inquiry and discovery require extra time, in part because of their constructivist nature. Within the constructivist model, a student builds on prior knowledge, experience, and images in order to build or construct new knowledge. Such a building process often requires more time and multiple exposure to the new concept. The extended class time available in the block schedule can encourage students to draw on prior knowledge and experience as they engage in new learning experiences without time pressure. These student-centered lessons also require students to use critical thinking skills as they make the transition from concrete to abstract thinking during well-planned learning experiences.

This chapter will provide a rationale for each teaching strategy, the general scope and sequence within a 90-minute lesson, and examples of each model in various core academic areas.

Students can actively engage in the exploration of new knowledge.

INQUIRY MODELS

Three different inquiry models are presented, each with its own syntax, but all with similar benefits to the learner. Inquiry Training, BSCS Inquiry, and Jurisprudential Inquiry have at their core the development of critical thinking and learner independence. All require students to engage in learning as active members. The extended block of classroom time can allow a teacher to plan for inquiry lessons that can be completed within one class meeting.

Inquiry Training

Robert Suchman's Inquiry Training Model (1962) is grounded in the belief that students can develop intellectual discipline and logical problem-solving abilities if provided with structured experiences that tap into their natural curiosity about the world. We all have the ability to inquire intuitively, but it is important to make the process of inquiry a conscious one so that we can analyze and improve our thinking.

The role of the teacher is to provide the students with a puzzling situation or discrepant event and to move them through five phases of inquiry that teach them a logical structure of inquiry. Once the rules of inquiry are established, students begin to ask yes/no questions of the teacher. These questions are a vehicle for gathering data. As students gain practice, they typically become more adept at asking questions from general to specific and are able to tune into clues given by preceding questions. As the questions become more specific, students are asked to offer hypotheses. These are discussed, and more questions are asked until the correct hypothesis is offered and validated. Finally, students are instructed to analyze the process of inquiry they just completed.

For students, the process allows them to "create knowledge" for themselves. This differs from a traditional lesson in which the knowledge is simply disseminated by the teacher to the student. Because the creation of knowledge requires more time than simple dissemination, the extended block offers both teacher and learner a golden opportunity for the development of several direct and indirect benefits.

Joyce et al. (1992) identify several values and attitudes that are directly promoted by the Inquiry Training Model. The primary benefits are in the acquisition of process skills (observing, collecting, and organizing data; identifying and controlling variables; formulating and testing hypotheses and explanations; inferring) and the development of strategies for creative inquiry through active, autonomous learning. Nurturant or indirect benefits include "verbal expressiveness, tolerance of ambiguity, persistence, logical thinking, and the attitude that all knowledge is tentative" (Joyce et al., 1992, p. 209).

The lesson begins with an explanation of the inquiry procedures and presentation of a discrepant event or puzzling situation in Phase One. You may want to consider the "rules of inquiry" listed in Table 4–1 to guide some early attempts in your classroom.

Once these rules are established, the discrepant event is presented and the questioning begins. Students take turns asking questions, and they may "pass" if they do not have a question at that time. We find it useful to record the questions and answers on a transparency, placing the initials of the student who offered the question next to the question. All questions should be accepted by the teacher. No judgment is made as to the quality or relevance of the questions during Phase Two

TABLE 4–1   Inquiry Training Rules

Rule 1	All questions must be asked in yes-or-no form. Invalid questions will be rephrased.
Rule 2	All questions and answers must be recorded by each student.
Rule 3	Every student will have an opportunity to ask one question before anyone has a chance to ask a second question.
Rule 4	When you are ready to form a hypothesis, indictate that a hypothesis will be offered. All students will record any hypothesis offered by the class.

(Data Gathering–Verification) or Phase Three (Data Gathering–Experimentation). The teacher simply records the question, provides an answer, or asks for the question to be reworded. During initial attempts, students may become sidetracked or stuck. At these points, you may decide to provide hints or clues to redirect the inquiry.

Once the students have arrived at the correct hypothesis, the teacher explains the concept in question. This is the only teacher-centered phase of the model. You can refer back to the questions and answers from Phase Two and Three and deliver a mini-lecture/discussion emphasizing information gathered by the class during the inquiry. Finally, the students are asked to analyze the inquiry process. For example, students can be told to label questions as either general or specific, relevant or irrelevant, clear or unclear. They may be asked to follow a logical path of thinking revealed by certain questions and not others. They can offer new questions that could have been asked. Table 4–2 summarizes the five steps of this inquiry method.

Consider the following example from a tenth-grade biology class. The students are presented with the following scenario:

> *Two twins identically dressed ski together at the same ski resort on the same day. At the end of the day, one of the twins suffers from hypothermia.*

This scenario represents the discrepant event. The students are given the inquiry rules, and the questioning process begins. Students may ask relevant or irrelevant questions, but the teacher must simply respond if they are phrased correctly. For example, students may ask:

TABLE 4–2   Five Phases of Inquiry Training

Phase One	The inquiry rules are presented and students are exposed to the puzzling situation or discrepant event.
Phase Two	Students ask yes/no questions, which are answered by the teacher, in order to begin gathering information.
Phase Three	Student questioning continues, and hypotheses are offered and examined by the class.
Phase Four	The correct hypothesis is discussed, and new content is taught that elaborates and explains the correct solution.
Phase Five	The students engage in an analysis of the path of inquiry they used.

1. Are they good skiers? YES
2. Did one have an accident and the other did not? NO
3. Are they identical twins? YES
4. Were they outside the same amount of time that day? YES
5. Was one sick before they went skiing and the other wasn't? NO
6. Was one taking medication? NO

Curious? This path of questioning is somewhat random. Some of these questions are "better" than others only from the perspective of the teacher who knows the answer! The process of questioning (gathering data) continues until the teacher senses that the students are getting close. Hypotheses are solicited, offered, and discussed. The students are always directed to look back at their record of questions/answers.

This particular inquiry was designed to teach students the effect of alcohol consumption on body temperature and hypothermia. The key question "Did one of the twins consume something that caused hypothermia?" would lead to more specific data gathering and experimentation (testing variables verbally) linking alcohol to hypothermia. Once confirmed, the teacher would present the mini-lecture on the content (Phase Four). Finally, students would be directed to analyze the inquiry in Phases One, Two, and Three, incorporating the new concepts learned in Phase Four.

Consider this example from social studies (Joyce et al., 1992, p. 206):

> *A map shows an island in the middle of a lake. The island is connected to the shore by a causeway made of stones piled on the bottom of the lake until the pile reached the surface. Then smoothed stones were laid down to make a road. The lake is surrounded by mountains, and the only flat land is near the lake. The island is covered with buildings whose walls are still standing, although the roofs are now gone. It is completely uninhabited.*

To reconstruct the historical and cultural events, acting as a team of anthropologists, the students must inquire about the inhabitants. There are several plausible explanations for this scenario. The path of student questions, their data collection and inference, will be guided by the teacher. The teacher can lead this inquiry in a number of possible directions: poor soil quality, disease, war, and so on.

When students are asked to analyze a particular literary work, they could begin by reading a passage and then engage in inquiry by directing questions to the teacher. For example, if the passage is particularly difficult and may generate multiple interpretations from students, the teacher may guide the inquiry toward one interpretation and then show students how other analyses may be made following a different set of questions. The literary analysis can be convergent if the teacher selects a work that has one clear interpretation, or divergent if the purpose of the critique is to foster several interpretations that require a defensible position based on a common set of criteria.

Other inquiry examples are presented in the subject-specific chapters that follow. Regardless of the subject matter, it is imperative that the discrepant event be just that. It must puzzle or challenge the students to move beyond concrete thinking. As teachers, we must allow students to struggle with the process at first and resist the temptation to "Just tell us the answer!" although they implore us to do so. Our experience has been that with practice, students improve their inquiry skills. Without any experience with structured inquiry, skills remain at an intuitive, subconscious level. Although this process takes time to develop, the short-term investment planned for the 90-minute block, revisited periodically with different topics, will pay long-term dividends.

BSCS Inquiry

The Biological Sciences Curriculum Study (BSCS) Inquiry Model uses an approach that teaches students to process information in ways similar to those used by a research biologist. First, problems are identified, and then a particular method is selected to solve the problem. Credited to Joseph Schwab (1965), the Invitations to Enquiry lessons engaged students with case studies developing either conceptual or methodological understanding. It is the use of the case studies that is particularly attractive within the extended block in the sciences and other core academic areas.

As students move through the area of investigation (Phase One), to structuring the problem (Phase Two), identification of the problem (Phase Three), and speculation/redesign (Phase Four), they gain experience with the process of research as a direct benefit. Joyce et al. (1992) also report nurturant benefits of open-mindedness, suspension of judgment, development of alternative solutions, and cooperative social skills:

> When students engage in this inquiry model, they must be welcomed into a community of seekers who use the best (empirical) techniques . . . the climate includes a certain degree of boldness as well as humility. The students need to hypothesize rigorously, challenge evidence, criticize, and so on. (Joyce et al., 1992, p. 136)

The emphasis on empirical evidence allows for the use of this model in many academic disciplines. Because Invitations to Enquiry clearly develops lessons for biology, the examples that follow illustrate how you may incorporate the BCSC model in nonscience academic areas. Table 4–3 illustrates the recommended sequence of this four-phase BSCS Inquiry model.

The use of opposing viewpoints presented clearly by two or more authors can serve as a springboard for inquiry in the social sciences and English. For example, students are exposed to two opposing editorials, from 1910–1914 American history, pro and con, on the entry of the United States into World War I. In Phase One, the students are exposed to the historical period in question. The problem is structured so that students must find empirical evidence to support or refute the entrance of the United States into the selected conflict (Phase Two). As students read the opposing views, they are to extract empirical evidence and critique the evidence presented by each of the authors (Phase Three). Finally, students are to offer

TABLE 4–3   BSCS Inquiry Sequence

Phase One	Students are presented with a situation that requires them to structure the problem.
Phase Two	Students compare and contrast their analysis from the first phase in order to reach consensus on the definition of the problem.
Phase Three	Students speculate on alternative ways to redesign or correct the problem in the investigation.
Phase Four	Students redesign or reconstruct the original work in order to improve the original work.

better empirical arguments, pro or con, and/or must offer alternative solutions to war involving the United States (Phase Four). Certainly, we hope that they would benefit from hindsight, but should they not make the connections to current world or domestic conditions, you may find this an excellent opportunity to make history relevant by helping them make these linkages.

In mathematics, students can be presented with an experimental design and hypothetical set of data collected from a laboratory. For example, an investigation into students' reaction times relative to a falling object would generate a data table indicating the individual reaction times of boys versus girls. If the students are attempting to determine, in one problem, if a significant difference exists between male and female reaction times, a simple descriptive analysis could be completed with the mean and standard deviation, and a simple t-test analysis would give the students an introduction to probability and statistics. The data are to be analyzed with reference to a list of hypotheses. Suppose that a lack of measurement control exists for determining accuracy of reaction time because the lab teams do not follow a standard procedure. Because the design is flawed, the analysis and conclusions will be flawed. Once the students review the laboratory procedure and data collection, they must identify the design flaw, explain how a new design will rectify the situation, and generate hypothetical or real data that can be analyzed using skills being learned in math class. Not only will the students gain experience with the research process, but they also will gain a real-life application of mathematics to science.

By applying the case study nature of the BSCS Inquiry Model, you can begin to create opportunities to develop research skills within the 90-minute block. The time frame for each phase will vary depending on the material selected for Phases One and Two. However, most of the 90-minute block should be devoted to Phase Three, in which students pick apart the flaws or inconsistencies with the case, and Phase Four, in which they offer new solutions or new designs. These critical research skills are not restricted to the sciences. They can be integrated between and among several academic areas. Such integration will be easier to accomplish if the block model selected allows for a common planning time between academic disciplines at the same grade level.

Jurisprudential Inquiry

This model has been included because of its potentially powerful impact on teaching students how to think systematically about contemporary social issues. Donald Oliver and James Shaver (1966) are credited with the development of a model that challenges students to view issues as public policy questions and to analyze alternative solutions to fundamental questions. Students are to assume the role of a Supreme Court judge as they listen to both sides of the issue, weigh evidence, assess the evidence with regard to the law, and make the best possible decision.

Oliver and Shaver identify three types of competence required to play this role. First, students must become familiar with the values framework embedded in the Constitution and the Declaration of Independence. Second, they must develop skills necessary for clarifying and resolving issues. Conflicts of values are likely to take one of three forms:

> The first kind of problem (value problem) involves clarifying which values or legal principles are in conflict and choosing among them. The second kind of problem (factual problem) involves clarifying facts around which the conflict has developed. The third kind of problem

(definitional problem) involves clarifying the meanings or uses of words which describes the controversy. (Oliver & Shaver, 1966, p. 89)

The third area of competence is the knowledge base within the political, social, economic fabric in which students need broad exposure to controversial issues in American society. Under this model, students explore issues in terms of a specific legal case rather than in terms of a general study of values. Eight basic social values are suggested as a legal-ethical framework: (1) Rule of Law, (2) Equal Protection under the Law, (3) Due Process, (4) Justice, (5) Preservation of Peace and Order, (6) Personal Liberty, (7) Separation of Powers, and (8) Local Control of Local Problems.

Six general problem areas are suggested, with several specific topics listed for each: (1) racial and ethnic conflict; (2) religious and ideological conflict; (3) security of the individual; (4) conflict among economic groups; (5) health, education, and welfare; and (6) security of the nation.

The general syntax of the jurisprudential model follows six phases, which can be viewed as two larger processes: analysis and argumentation. The extended block can allow for the class to complete the inquiry in one or two class meetings, depending on the depth of the case under investigation. During Phase One, the orientation to the case, the teacher introduces the material and reviews the facts of the case. In Phase Two, identifying the issues, students synthesize facts into public policy issue(s), select the policy for investigation and discussion, identify values and value conflicts, and recognize factual and definitional questions. Phase Three, taking positions, completes the analysis block and requires students to take a position and state the basis of the position in terms of the social value or consequences. One 90-minute block may be adequate for the completion of this analysis process.

Once each student or team of students has articulated a position in Phase Three, the argumentation process begins. Phase Four, exploring stances and patterns of argumentation, requires students to establish the point at which a value is violated, prove the potential desirable or undesirable outcomes, clarify the conflict through the use of analogies, and set priorities. With this phase, you follow a Socratic style by challenging the position of the student or team. The function of the teacher in this powerful examination of student positions is to question the student's relevance, consistency, specificity, and clarity. The teacher's questions

are designed to push students' thinking about their stances and to help them learn:

Does it hold up well against positions reflecting alternative views?
Is it consistent across many situations?
Are the reasons for maintaining the position relevant?
Are the factual assumptions valid?
What are the consequences of this position?
Will the student hold on to this stance in spite of its consequences?

(Joyce et al., 1992, p. 76)

Phase Five encourages students to refine and qualify the positions following the Socratic dialogue with the teacher. Phase Six provides another test of the position by examining the factual assumptions behind it to determine if they hold up under rigorous challenge. Throughout the argumentation in Phases Four, Five, and Six, the teacher must emphasize that the merits of the case are being challenged, not the students themselves. Table 4–4 provides a general overview of this six-phase sequence.

TABLE 4–4   Jurisprudential Inquiry

Analysis Block

Phase One	Students are oriented to the selected case to include review of pertinent facts.
Phase Two	Students determine related public policy issues, focus on one issue, and relate it to value conflicts.
Phase Three	Students take a position on the issue selected.

Argumentation Block

Phase Four	Students present their position and the teacher follows a Socratic dialogue.
Phase Five	Students refine and qualify their original stance.
Phase Six	Teacher challenges the new position by examining the factual foundation of the argument.

THE LEARNING CYCLE

Moving students from concrete to formal or abstract thinking requires the frequent use of concrete experience and the opportunity to apply concepts. The learning cycle as an instructional strategy was developed in 1962 by Myron Atkin and Robert Karplus at the University of California at Berkeley, and later modified by Karplus as part of the Science Curriculum Improvement Study (SCIS) and for Development of Reasoning Workshops (Karplus, 1977). Several subsequent modifications have been made over the past two decades. The model is grounded in Piagetian principles of cognitive development, which will be briefly discussed. The three-phase syntax will be developed, and examples from science, mathematics, social studies, and English will be presented.

Consider the following pairs of statements, and select the statement from each pair with which you are more inclined to agree.

- **A.** Intelligence is the ability to adapt to environmental change.
- **B.** Intelligence is mental age divided by chronological age.

- **A.** Knowledge is a copy of reality.
- **B.** Knowledge is an adaptation of cognitive structures to reality.

- **A.** Learning is a modification of behavior due to experience.
- **B.** Learning is the modification of cognitive structures due to activity.

- **A.** Learning is the process of taking in concepts that represent reality.
- **B.** Learning is the process of restructuring existing concepts so that they are more appropriate explanations of reality.

- **A.** Teaching is the presentation of material in a logical order.
- **B.** Teaching is engaging the learner with materials that require cognitive adaptation.

From each pair of statements, one statement is aligned with Piaget's theory of cognitive development (A, B, B, B, B). Some fundamental differences in views of teaching, learning, knowledge, and intelligence distinguish Piaget's theory from more traditional ones.

High school students enter our classrooms with cognitive structures at an initial level of equilibrium. They hold significant preconceptions and misconceptions about how and why things work they way they do. Although they are developmentally capable of formal operations between ages 12 and 15, they often mystify us with their inability to perform tasks that require abstract thinking. If we rethink the way we teach, we may find that we assume the ability to make the leap from concrete to formal thinking because, within our discipline, we have been doing it for a long time. In reality, even though learners are capable of formal operational thinking, if the concept is new and they have not had prior concrete experience, there will be a reversion to concrete operations until adequate experience has been provided. Once it is provided, cognitive adaptation can occur.

The process of cognitive adaptation involves five steps. First, learners have a cognitive structure at an initial level of equilibrium. How they think "works" under the circumstances and conditions of learning. Next, they encounter a situation that requires intelligent behavior beyond the present cognitive structure. In other words, you have challenged them with a problem that cannot be resolved using their current cognitive structure. Step Three is cognitive disequilibrium: the teachable moment when the learner must adapt or revert (or give up!). To move from disequilibrium, the learner must adapt the cognitive structures through assimilation and accommodation. Finally, a new cognitive structure is established at a new, higher level of equilibrium.

The learning cycle embraces Piagetian theory and provides for a simple and eloquent planning structure that incorporates student-centered activity during the first and third phases. It is also well suited for use during the extended block because it allows for ample practice with concrete examples and phenomena before moving to abstract application activities.

Students who use concrete reasoning patterns require a reference to objects, events, or actions in order to undertake logical reasoning. They are unaware of the inconsistencies in their own thought patterns. By contrast, students using formal reasoning do so conceptually using theories, hypothetical constructs, axioms, and indirect relationships. They are aware of inconsistencies in their thinking because of their ability to analyze their thought processes.

Like the inquiry models presented earlier, the learning cycle attempts to create cognitive dissonance, disequilibrium, or "What is going on here?" in the mind of the student. The learning cycle gives the student opportunities to experience concepts and principles in a concrete manner at first. These concepts are presented in a concrete fashion. During the exploration phase, the teacher may select a hands-on activity, a demonstration, video clip, data set, illustration, or other mechanism to show students the concept in a direct manner.

This is a well-structured exploration that can be completed within one extended-block class period. Your job is to plan and set the stage. Whatever method is selected for this phase, it must be concrete. Your role is that of a facilitator. If properly planned, student preconceptions and misconceptions are uncovered as they attempt to answer fundamental questions during the exploration phase.

It is imperative that students try to answer teacher-selected questions in their own language. Where traditional teaching would define a myriad of terms in isolated, abstract ways, the learning cycle allows students to assign meaning to the exploration without using proper vocabulary at first. The teacher should keep a written list of student responses to the key exploration questions to be used in the second phase of the learning cycle.

During Phase Two, you introduce or invent the concepts, skills, and principles for the students. Critical to this phase (invention) is to use the student language from Phase One and translate it into the correct language in Phase Two. For example:

- If the student observes a white light passing through a prism and says, "It splits into different colors," you would record this and use it in Phase Two to introduce refraction.
- If a student in a geometry class explores the relationship between area and circumference of a circle and says, "As one gets bigger, so does the other," although it is an obvious observation, the teacher accepts it and can use it to develop the direct relationship in the equation: Both are in the numerator because it is a direct relationship.

$$A = \pi r^2$$
$$C = \pi D = 2 \pi r^2$$

- If students read a persuasive antiwar speech written during the Vietnam War and are asked to list the ways the author tries to convince the reader, they do not have to know in advance what to look for. The variety of answers provided by the students are listed by the teacher, then discussed, and finally categorized under persuasive technique headings.

Whenever the input from the students leaves significant gaps, the teacher fills the gaps by pointing out what students did not include in their answers to key questions from Phase One. Phase Two is similar to a teacher-centered lecture/discussion. The content is directly taught, but it is always related to the student experience from Phase One. The experience with the concept is concrete, and the teacher invents the vocabulary to flesh out the concept.

During Phase Three (exploration), students are required to apply the concept to a new situation:

- In the light refraction example, students may be experimenting with light refraction in different media.
- In geometry, they may be developing pi as a constant relationship in circles regardless of the radius.
- In English, once students have learned from exploration and invention how to categorize persuasive techniques, they can analyze other speeches of the same time period, or write their own using selected techniques.

The learning cycle departs significantly from didactic forms of instruction. The teacher begins by providing the student with concrete experience with the concept or skill, free from vocabulary. Students actively engage in the exploration and answer fundamental questions designed to create a dissonance. During Phase Two, the teacher solicits student ideas in student language and invents the concept, transforming student language into concepts and principles, filling any conceptual gaps. Once students have completed the exploration and invention phases, they are required to apply the concepts and skills to a new situation. This discovery phase allows them to make the transition from concrete to formal thinking. The role of the teacher returns to that of the facilitator, requiring students to use the correct language and concepts emphasized in Phases One and Two.

A 90-minute block permits the completion of the learning cycle through the completion of Phase Three in most cases. The transition between phases is uninterrupted. Although this model was originally designed for the sciences, it has excellent potential in nonscience classrooms as well. The keys to learning cycle success include careful structuring of concrete experiences in Phase One that require students to focus on fundamental questions, the use of a written record of student ideas from Phase One during the invention of concepts in Phase Two, and finally the opportunity to practice the skill in a new situation during the discovery (application) activity in Phase Three. As with the inquiry model, other examples of learning cycle lessons are presented in the subject-specific chapters.

The use of inquiry models and learning cycle lesson designs within the extended block allows students to engage in meaningful higher level thinking skills through hands-on and minds-on activity. Use of these models is possible within a traditional class period but is better served by the extended class period because there is ample time to fully develop student thinking without interruption.

■ 5
Incorporating Study Skills

ALL SECONDARY TEACHERS think their content area is the most interesting and probably the most important. It is therefore a continuing source of frustration that students seem to go through the motions of learning the content instead of appreciating the value and fascination of the subject: "If only my students could learn to love math as I do."

Before students can learn to love a particular subject, they must be comfortable with the subject. They need to be able to handle the related material on their own, without direct assistance from a teacher. Independence in learning brings students to an appreciation of the subject. Unfortunately, in the time crunch to deliver content, we often don't tend to the nurturing of skills that will lead students to be independent learners.

Content-area study skills can serve as the tools to move students from teacher dependence to independence while developing an interest in subject matter material. In-class tasks and homework assignments are easier and thus more often finished when students can complete these projects without reliance on the teacher for step-by-step instructions. Study skills help students meet with frequent success in the content areas. Aren't we all more interested in what we can do successfully?

The extended-block period is ripe with opportunities to present and apply content-area study skills. The longer chunks of time available each day allow students not only to learn the content material, but also to acquire the skills necessary to pursue more about the content on their own. Independent study skills that are productive encourage students to interact with content material more frequently and at a higher level of understanding. Student learning moves from rote recall at literal levels of understanding to obtain a passing grade on the next exam, to analysis, synthesis, and critical thinking, developing motivation to learn more. Thus, the development of study skills within the extended class period enhances student learning throughout the academic year.

Mastery of successful study skills in any one class saves time for students and teachers who wish to apply those skills in any other class. Because content-area study skills are easy adapted to multiple curriculum areas, students can carry these strategies from one class to another and meet with similar levels of success. There is no need for all teachers to spend a great deal of time teaching study skills to their students. If a student can adjust reading rate in the science classroom, that same student can readjust reading rate for the English literature experience. A skill learned in one area in this way benefits students and teacher in all areas. Teachers are making a long-term investment that will reap benefits across curriculum areas and throughout the school year.

ESSENTIAL CONTENT

Teachers and students alike can easily be overwhelmed by the breadth of any academic content area, and extended-block periods do not reduce this amount of material. The secondary curriculum seems to grow almost exponentially each and every year. Teachers feel administrative and societal pressures to teach more and faster. Students feel parental and teacher pressure to learn as many facts as they can. The extended block allows students and teachers to move beyond this approach to the bulging curriculum by providing longer single periods of time to examine the essential content of any one subject. Teachers can reassume the position of decision makers as they have the opportunities to investigate content information thoroughly within individual class meetings.

Stepping back and carefully examining any content curriculum results in a differentiation of the essential content, which is definitely necessary for students to know, from information that is peripheral. Teachers select the essential content of their subject when they attempt to match their curriculum with their text. When teachers plan class instruction, they are, in effect, planning to pull out and emphasize that essential content for students. They are identifying what is important for students to know. This focus on the essential content can allow students truly to learn, remember, understand, and apply material in any content area. Once this essential content is mastered, the road to extended aspects of the subject is wide open. All the students need are the study skills tools to help them travel that road, independently.

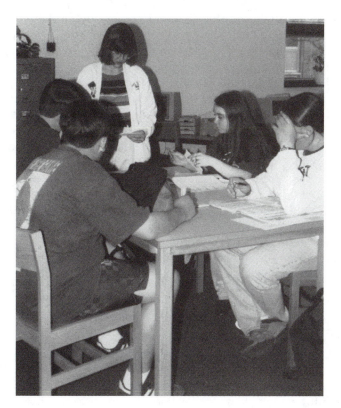

The extended-block period provides time for students to practice newly acquired skills.

GUIDED TEXTBOOK READING

How many of you have distributed textbooks to your students and said, "Please read Chapter 3 for tomorrow"? How many of your students have grumbled, looked at you as if you had spoken in tongues, or rolled their eyes? Have you considered that it may not be just that these students don't *want* to read Chapter 3, but that they aren't exactly sure *how* to read Chapter 3? Perhaps giving students a hint about the chapter, making it somewhat familiar and a bit predictable, clarifying what you expect of them as they read would ease their confusion. If you want students to read, you only need to give them some guidance in how to read successfully.

Every textbook has a different approach to presenting information dependent upon the authors, the subject matter, and the intended audience. Students need to know how to identify the approach used in your particular textbook. Techniques such as Guided Previewing, Prediction Guides, and Focus Questions give students reading skills adaptable to most content texts. The extended-block period provides enough time to present and practice these skills during class while simultaneously exploring the essential content. Once these skills are mastered, students can apply them to independent reading assignments for any teacher.

Guided Previewing

Students don't often come to our classes with giddy expectation or an anticipation of happy surprise with the content to be explored. They come to our classes expecting us to tell them what we want them to learn. They expect us to guide them in this learning whether it occurs through cooperative learning activities, lectures, or assigned reading.

Before assigning any textbook reading, no matter its length, preview the material with the students. An organized preview can assist students in focusing on the content at hand. It encourages them to draw on their current knowledge about the content, and it sets the stage for adding to that knowledge. Previewing requires only 5 or 10 minutes of your class time and can take several forms.

Graves, Cooke, and Laberge (1983) suggest a four-step approach to previewing textual material with secondary students. First, the teacher presents an introduction to the reading assignment. Second, the teacher provides important background information which students may not have. Third, a previously written brief summation of the content is read aloud. Fourth, students are given purpose-setting questions to be answered at the conclusion of the reading. Table 5–1 provides an example of this type of preview for a social studies lesson.

Prediction/Anticipation Guide

Prediction Guides, sometimes referred to as Anticipation Guides, assist students in making connections between what they already know and what they are going to be reading in the text. They help students set purposes for reading that provide for increased comprehension of the essential content in that text as students assimilate new information into what they knew before reading. This integration of students' background knowledge with textual information bridges the gap between student and text. Prediction/Anticipation Guides involve several components, each separate from but building upon the others as they help students see the purpose for

TABLE 5–1   Four-Step Preview

Step #1—Introduction

We are beginning a unit on the study of the American Civil War. During the next week, we'll examine the political climate prior to the war, consider the causes of the war, and explore the significant people and events of the antebellum period. Today we will learn the state of America in the years immediately prior to the Civil War.

Step #2—Background Information

Most people think slavery was the cause of the Civil War, and it was a contributing factor. But there were many other very political reasons that were direct causes as much as that of the actual enslavement of people. Among them were the fugitive slave law, states' rights, and the election of Abraham Lincoln.

Step #3—Brief Summation

The issue of slavery grew stronger by 1850, and debates raged among the American people and their political leaders. As settlers moved west, a decision needed to be made concerning slavery within the new territories. This led to the ultimate question of individual states' rights about slavery and other things. Because all states did not agree, discussion turned to secession and the dissolving of the union. As Abraham Lincoln took office, virtually without southern support, the southern states looked toward seceding and forming a government of their own.

Step #4—Purpose-Setting Questions

Now you'll read the section of your text titled "Setting the Stage for War." While you are reading, pay particular attention to: (1) What political leaders did to try to find a compromise on the issues related to slavery, (2) how northerners and southerners differed in their reactions to the Fugitive Slave Law, and (3) how the division of the nation was demonstrated in the election of 1856.

---

reading, focus on the essential content within the reading, and increase an interest in the reading.

The following steps will help you to prepare an effective guide for your students:

1. Examine the section to be read. Clarify what you consider the essential content, and look for connections between that essential information and what students may already know.
2. Prepare a brief introduction or overview of the section to be read. Write this on the top of the guide.
3. Write clear directions that encourage students to consider the subject under study.
4. Create statements that address the content but draw on students' existing knowledge. Write these in a list format under the directions.

To illustrate a content example, Table 5–2 shows a Prediction/Anticipation Guide for Literature: "Just Lather, That's All" by Hernando Tellez.

Prediction/Anticipation Guides require careful teacher preparation before class, then a fading during class as students personalize the task set before them on the basis of their background knowledge. Your job moves from that of a highly visible and directive leader when developing and presenting the Prediction/Anticipation Guide to that of a participant observer, moderator, and facilitator as

TABLE 5–2 Prediction/Anticipation Guide for Literature

Directions: In the blanks, mark whether or not you agree (+) or disagree (–) with each statement.

I	Group	Author	
_____	_____	_____	1. It's O.K. to kill one to save the lives of many.
_____	_____	_____	2. Decision making is easy if you know what you stand for.
_____	_____	_____	3. Cruelty deserves cruelty.
_____	_____	_____	4. People avoid going to places where they know they'll be harmed.
_____	_____	_____	5. Hate is more powerful than logic.
_____	_____	_____	6. When we are members of a group, we are willing to put aside our own beliefs to follow the rules of a group.

Source: B. Rodriguez-McCleary & M. J. Vaught, *Anticipation Prediction Guide* (Fairfax, VA: Fairfax County Schools, 1994). Used with permission.

students employ the guide. Table 5–3 summarizes the steps for using the Prediction/Anticipation Guide.

The Prediction/Anticipation Guide provides meaningful discussion in small groups to analyze student views and to practice consensus building before material is read. The author's view is considered in light of each individual's own experiences and through critical reflection on the text piece.

During the extended-block period, the Prediction/Anticipation Guide allows you the opportunity to observe all students and engage in individual or small-group dialogues. The greater amount of time in the extended-block period allows the students to move through the entire process without interruption. A piece of essential content can be introduced, read, and critically analyzed independently and with peers. The extended block provides the time the teacher needs to bring closure to the process.

Cooperative Reading Guide (COOR Guide)

Adapted from Wood's collaborative listening-viewing guide (1992), the COOR Guide has been developed to assist students when they are to take notes about the

TABLE 5–3 Prediction/Anticipation Guide

1. Students first complete the guide individually according to your instructions.
2. In small groups, students share their responses and explain why they responded in the way they did.
3. Each small group arrives at a consensus after discussing each member's responses.
4. Each student reads the assigned text silently.
5. After reading, students reconsider their initial responses on the guide considering how the author would have responded.
6. In small groups, students discuss what they feel the author's responses would have been providing justification from the text material.

TABLE 5–4   COOR Worksheet

1. What is a predator–prey relationship?

2. How can we study changes in these types of relationships over time?

3. How is competition related to the predator–prey relationship?

4. Use the graph on page 130 to summarize what appears to be happening to each population over the 40-year time span. Then predict what may happen over the next five years, and justify your prediction with information from the chapter.

essential content from their text reading. It directs students through the textual material so they are able to choose the core information that is important to the essential content expected to be learned.

There are five steps in using the COOR Guide with secondary students.

1. *Overview of the material for the students:* In this step the teacher provides a brief overview of the content information to be read, emphasizing the essential content. This is usually done orally.
2. *Guiding worksheet:* Students are then given a prepared worksheet to use when reading the text material assigned.
3. *Reading and taking notes:* As students read the material, they individually write down appropriate information as guided by the worksheet.
4. *Peer collaboration:* When students have finished exploring the text and taking notes, they meet with one or two of their classmates to share the information each has selected. At this time, students may edit their notes based on what classmates have discussed.
5. *Information confirmation:* Students now apply the information they have gathered. This can be done through whole-class discussion, writing summary essays, developing concept maps, or oral presentations.

Table 5–4 provides an example of a COOR Guide worksheet for a biology class. The students have been given an oral overview of the text material by the teacher. In this overview it was noted the reading assignment would illustrate predator–prey relationships, food webs, and human influences on these relationships.

The COOR Guide helps students and teacher make efficient use of both text material and class time. The extended class time provided by the block schedule allows a complete application of the COOR Guide and investigation of a complete piece of content. Students are moved from introduction of new information through exploration of the information to the application of that information, all under the supervision of the teacher. Completing this process within one class period allows the teacher to make immediate assessment of student progress with the content material so the next day's instruction can be responsive to their progress.

Textbook Activity Guide

The Textbook Activity Guide (TAG) (Davey, 1986) helps students monitor their own progress while reading a content text. Students work in pairs to examine the content and to self-monitor the process used to read the content and their progress with the content. Questions in the TAG direct the students to appropriate pages in the text to help them locate essential content information.

In developing the TAG, the teacher determines strategies and corresponding strategy codes as well as self-monitoring categories and corresponding self-monitoring codes for students to use when reading assigned content material. The strategies are selected based on the content material under examination. The teacher then identifies the learning objectives specific to the lesson and locates sections of the text that contain content relevant to those objectives. Reading directions are then written to guide students through the content reading. Students work with partners to use the strategies identified and monitor their own understanding of the content.

Davey (1986) provides the following suggestions for strategies and strategy codes and self-monitoring categories and self-monitoring codes:

Strategies and Strategy Codes

D	Discuss with your partner.
WR	Provide a written response on your own.
Skim	Read quickly for the given purpose and discuss with your partner.
Map	Create a semantic map of the information.
P	Predict with your partner.

Self-Monitoring Decisions and Self-Monitoring Codes

+	I understand this information.
?	I'm not sure if I understand.
x	I do not understand and I need to restudy.

To demonstrate content application, Table 5–5 shows a TAG developed for an Algebra text for secondary students.

TABLE 5–5   TAG for Algebra

Strategies

D	Discuss with your partner.
WR	Provide a written response on your own.
Skim	Read quickly for the given purpose and discuss with your partner.
Map	Create a semantic map of the information.
P	Predict with your partner.

Self-Monitoring Decisions

+		I understand this information.
?		I'm not sure if I understand.
x		I do not understand and I need to restudy.
_____	P	Pages 176–181: Look over the titles, subtitles, and illustrations. What do you think you will learn about in this section?
_____	D	Page 176: Read the two paragraphs in the introduction and the example. Discuss the three steps you need to use in solving the equations with your partner.
_____	WR	Pages 177–178. Read the first problem. In your notebook, solve the problem, noting each step in the process.
_____	WR, D	Share your written process with your partner explaining each step you used and why you selected each step.

In the extended-block period, the TAG strategy gives teachers the opportunity to guide students of different reading abilities through essential content material. Detailed examination of the content, guided reading of the textbook, cooperation with peers, and reflection of personal progress are all addressed with teacher guidance in one extended class meeting. The length of the extended-block period allows students to complete the entire process maximizing successful interaction with the essential content.

GRASP

GRASP (Hayes, 1989) is a guided reading and summarizing procedure developed to help students recall content information. By directing students in organizing the text material, GRASP increases their efficiency in reading and remembering essential content presented in their textbook.

In this procedure, the teacher begins by carefully preparing students to summarize. Using short factual text material is helpful in preparing students to get ready to learn this skill. The teacher discusses summarizing and demonstrates the process for students. The teacher also reminds students that their summaries will be written in small groups to allow them to generate and receive ideas to include.

Next, the teacher has the students read the actual text assignment and notes that they are reading in order to be able to recall as much of the information as they can. This will require slow, careful reading of the essential content. When students have completed the reading, the class generates a list of the information they can remember. The teacher can then have students return to the text material to locate any important information that may have been neglected. This is added to the class list.

Students are reminded they will use the class list information as the beginning of their summaries and to consider only the most important information, eliminating unnecessary details. Students may also combine pieces of information when creating their summaries.

The teacher then helps students organize the list information into major topics, reflecting those used in the texts. A class discussion can help students understand these categories and consider the relationships among them in preparation for writing the final summaries.

Teacher modeling is important as students use the list of information and categories developed to create written summaries. The teacher selects the first topic area and, using the class list, writes a sentence for it. Students then help the teacher create the next sentence, again based on the list information. Students complete the summary individually by referring to the class list and sentences written collaboratively. As summaries are written, students are encouraged to share their progress with their small group. At this point they are able to revise their individual work based on feedback from their peers.

The amount of time available in the extended-block period allows the teacher and students to complete the entire GRASP strategy. The teacher can model for students, a step often skipped by content teachers in the interest of time. This modeling is crucial in moving students toward independence with content reading. Students can participate in large- and small-group discussions, thus benefiting from multiple perspectives and immediate feedback. Students can write complete summaries of content material in direct reflection of content material just read. By completing the entire procedure within one class period, the students are prepared for the next step, whether it is further content development, an exam, a written report, or an oral presentation. The teacher can move forward knowing students have a grasp of the essential content of the subject.

K-W-L

The K-W-L technique (Ogle, 1986) capitalizes on what students already know about the content material (K), explores information they would like to know about the subject (W), and provides for examination of what was actually learned (L). This technique provides a motivating approach to guide students from pre-reading, through the actual reading of the text, and into reflection on growth as a result of reading the text.

As the name suggests, the strategy has three major steps:

1. The teacher provides a brief oral overview of the content material to be studied. The teacher presents a large chart with three columns, labeled K (Know), W (Want to Know), and L (Learned).
2. Students are asked to brainstorm any information they already have about the subject to be studied. As responses are given, the teacher writes them in the column labeled K.
3. The teacher then asks students to share what they would like to know about the subject. Teachers may need to encourage students to consider concepts instead of factual information. As responses are given, the teacher writes them in the column labeled W. (Some teachers prefer K-N-L because high school students relate more readily to the question of what they *need* to know than to what they *want* to know.)
4. The students are then directed to read the text section independently.
5. Students look back to the W column of the K-W-L chart and share responses to the issues identified. Their responses are entered under the L column. The teacher can use this time to supplement responses given and encourage students to expand on information provided.

Because the K-W-L strategy takes students through content materials in a step-by-step process, it is particularly effective in the extended-block period. When students have the time to prepare for reading, do the reading, and reflect upon the reading without interruption, their comprehension increases. The extended block allows this process to occur uninterrupted, thus maximizing constructive time on task. Teachers can monitor the process and assess the product allowing for increased attention to proactive planning.

Though most frequently used with whole groups of students, the K-W-L strategy can be applied to smaller cooperative groups and even to individual students who are ready to operate more independently than some of their classmates and can draw on their own schema and set their own learning goals. Table 5–6 provides a blank K-W-L chart adaptable to all content areas.

TABLE 5–6   Blank K-W-L Chart

K	W	L
What We Know	What We Want to Know	What We Learned

GRAPHIC ORGANIZERS/SEMANTIC MAPS

Graphic organizers, also called semantic maps, are used to provide visual representation of essential content information. By providing students with a diagram of concepts and relationships, graphic organizers provide order to the essential content of any subject. And because graphic organizers focus on essential content, extraneous information is eliminated right away.

Graphic organizers are easily adapted across curriculum areas. They can be used to introduce new material, to review previously studied information, to begin the exploration of upcoming material, and to make connections between past information and newly acquired content. Graphic organizers require students to restructure given information in an orderly manner, thereby encouraging critical thinking of content and active involvement of students. When applied to reading content material, they allow students to consider pieces of the information in isolation and to examine how the individual pieces fit together within the concept.

Most graphic organizers fall into the categories of linear or hierarchical, but if the relationships shown within the organizing diagram are logical, the graphic organizer will work. Some organizers may therefore seem circular or even chronological. As long as the resulting diagram shows appropriate connections among the pieces of the content, the format is flexible. Figure 5–1 shows two graphic organizers created from the same information for a social studies lesson about the Panama Canal.

As a tool to facilitate understanding of the concepts surrounding content information, graphic organizers have proved to be quite effective. Given the time in an extended-block schedule, they are even more efficient in completing an exploration of content. Students are able to read, discuss, and critically consider textual information, and then, within the same class period, demonstrate their understanding of what has just been studied. The teacher can therefore immediately assess student progress, clarify misunderstandings, reinforce material understood, and prepare for the next bit of information. With the time provided in the longer class period, the graphic organizer effectively moves students from superficial reading to in-depth understanding of any content material.

FIGURE 5–1 Graphic Organizers for the Panama Canal

PEOPLE	PROBLEMS	COSTS
President T. Roosevelt	Disease	Human lives
Col. George Goethals	Yellow fever	$400 million
Dr. W.C. Gorgas	Malaria	
	Bubonic plague	
	Colombia	
	Clayton-Bulwer Treaty	

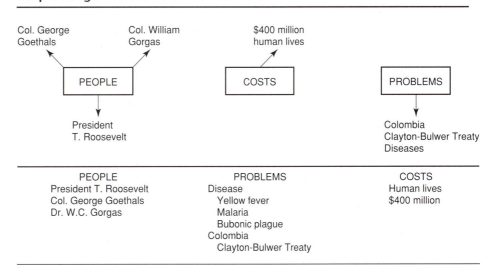

SUMMARY

We would all agree that student interest is an important factor in their learning. Stimulating that interest can lay the foundation for positive interaction with any subject. Using study skills strategies helps the classroom teacher to provide the in-depth experiences with their texts that build this foundation. Integrated in the class time provided by the extended-block schedule, study skills instruction facilitates the ability of secondary teachers to address fully the essential content necessary on an ongoing basis.

 # PART TWO

Longer periods allow students to tackle more meaningful class work.

■ 6
Teaching English

WE FIRST THINK of the extended-block schedule as tailor-made for science, art, music, industrial technology, and other laboratory-based courses. However, this scheduling innovation brings several advantages to the English instructor as well.

FOUR ADVANTAGES IN THE ENGLISH CLASSROOM

The first advantage offered to the English teacher is the reduction in teaching load. Teaching load continues to be a weakness and an area of concern for English teachers as evidenced by the most recent national survey of 650 schools conducted by the Center for Literature Teaching and Learning (Langer, 1992). The study revealed that only 28 percent of public secondary schools could agree that their teaching loads fell within the 100-student limit set by the National Council of Teachers of English. Not surprisingly, public schools identified as excellent in English instruction were also those reporting lighter teaching loads.

The extended-block schedule in which the teacher sees three classes per day reduces the teaching load for most teachers to or below the 100-student limit. This reduced teaching load is crucial for English teachers, who bear the primary responsibility for teaching students to write. Not only does the block provide extended time for the writing workshop format and for serious attention to the components of process writing, but it also allows the teacher more time to conference with students about their work and to evaluate writing samples.

The second advantage of the extended block in the English classroom is that it allows enough time to plan seriously for an integrated approach to the teaching of language arts. Throughout time, educators have expressed concern about the need for integrating personal life experience with learning and about lack of student enjoyment in learning. In the early 1900s, John Dewey highlighted the isolated nature of schooling and the lack of retention by students. He encouraged problem solving, shared decision making, learning through experience, and making links between learning experiences and the students' own past and future experiences. As English teachers, most of us would readily agree that reading, writing, listening, and speaking are interdependent, but too few of us have really been able to integrate that belief into our curricula.

More recently, the integrated, holistic approach to teaching language arts has been acknowledged again for its long-term learning results (Maxwell & Meiser, 1997). Research during the 1980s and 1990s into cognitive processes, learning styles, teaching methods, and strategies for effective learning has again emphasized the necessity for a more holistic approach to education. Maxwell and Meiser's tenets of such a holistic approach to education are summarized in Table 6–1.

Many of us worry that this integrated approach means a breakdown in the traditional classroom strategies and structure that have proved effective before. But this integration does not mean that the traditional teaching strategies of lecture,

TABLE 6–1   The Major Tenets of a Holistic Language Arts Philosophy

- The student is an active participant within a community of learners.
- The teacher structures and facilitates learning, but does not "hand it out."
- Language is best learned through authentic communication and meaningful contexts, not through exercises about it.
- Language occurs holistically, not in small parts to be put together like Legos or building blocks.
- Oral and written language are integrated, positively influencing one another.
- Students, not subject matter, are the heart of a classroom.
- The teacher recognizes and respects the individual abilities and unique needs of students.
- Classroom environment fosters risk taking, where errors are linked to growth.
- Students learn through constructing meaning from the world around them.
- Students work both cooperatively and independently.

Source: R. J. Maxwell & M. J. Meiser, *Teaching English in Middle and Secondary Schools,* 2nd ed. (Upper Saddle River, NJ: Merrill, 1997), pp. 7–8. Used with permission.

guided discussion, literary analysis, and the study of grammatical structures have no place, nor does it promote a classroom without structure. It does not mean that students dictate the curriculum. Expectations of high-quality student work can and should be upheld; evaluations of students must reflect these expectations. This holistic concept does mean that teachers will plan for meaningful student involvement, which draws on their past experiences, their personal interests and concerns, and the real world around them. It also means linking those elements to the context of literature, writing, listening, and speech so that students will become empowered through their understanding of and skill in using the various facets of the English curriculum.

The third advantage that the extended-block schedule offers English teachers is the time to plan in greater depth and to reflect on the types of activities best suited to strengthening their students' understanding and use of the language.

In contrast, many of us who are currently operating on the seven- or eight-period day with 125+ students have learned to rely on the textbook as a base for instruction. Many of us have largely given up the decision-making process and allowed the textbook to determine the areas of language arts to be emphasized in our classrooms. Overworked teachers trying to give their preparation periods and after-school hours to the time-consuming task of evaluating student writing have neither planning time nor energy left over to create whole lessons based on their own interpretation of their students' needs.

Additionally, once we begin to follow the chapter-by-chapter dictates of the textbook, teaching the various facets of English quickly becomes compartmentalized. For instance, it is not unusual to observe whole class periods dedicated to textbook grammar exercises isolated from meaningful content and united only by the grammatical concept illustrated in each sentence. Even the sentence examples within an exercise do not relate contextually to each other. The explanations, student completion of exercises, and subsequent teacher review of that work seem to have little or no relevance to the lives and experiences of the students, to the literature emphasized in the course, nor to the writing that students have done or will do after grammar has been "covered." The study of the grammar, conventions, and mechanics of the language too often exists in isolation. With added preparation time, we can prepare lessons that highlight important grammatical concepts in relation to a literary selection or that are drawn from the students' own writing.

The extended block allows a flexibility in the teaching of literature that occurs too seldom with the anthology approach. Currently, many teachers follow the chronological format of their literature anthology even though they may see more pertinent and helpful organizational patterns for their students. An extended-block schedule will provide time to develop the thought-provoking questions or the student-centered activities that lead to deeper learning.

In the Center for Literature Teaching and Learning national survey (1990), teachers indicated that 50 to 78 percent of a student's time in the English classroom is dedicated to the study of literature. Teachers reaffirmed the traditional organization of genre study in grades 7–10, American literature in grade 11, and British literature in grade 12; they also listed whole-class discussion as the primary means of instruction regardless of genre, with "no changes in content or approaches to the teaching of literature in their departments during the next few years" (Langer, 1992, p. 7).

The growing interest in extended-block scheduling may, however, provide the time, the lighter teaching loads, and the opportunity for dialogue and reflection necessary if teachers wish to plan a variety of approaches to the teaching of language arts in the secondary school. Instead of using the textbook as the curriculum determiner, this scheduling format may encourage teachers to use their own expertise as a base for diagnosing exactly which content areas are most needed and most beneficial to each class. Teachers should not worry that textbooks might be abolished in a holistic environment; instead, they will be useful resources to be

TABLE 6–2   Summary of the Standards for the English Language Arts

Reading	The Standards encourage us to have our students experience as many types of literary, print, film, and electronic media as possible and develop their ability to use several strategies in order to understand what they read and to apply an increased understanding of universal themes and the human condition to other texts, to their own lives, and to societal issues.
Speech	Students need to learn to employ many forms of spoken language so that messages that they communicate may effectively reach many types of audiences.
Writing	Students need to learn to appreciate and apply the writing process to communicate effectively for a variety of purposes and to modify their written communication to address new purposes.
Research	Students must learn to think critically and to problem-solve through data searches, information analysis, and the presentation of their conclusions in an effective manner to reach their target audience. They must learn to use print and nonprint sources as well as electronic information sources to gather information as they explore possible solutions.
Structure	Students need to employ structural elements and the conventions of the language effectively in spoken and written communication.
Cultural Awareness	Students need to understand the various cultures influencing our society and to appreciate the languages, dialects, and ethnic contributions of a diverse population. Those students for whom English is a second language need to utilize their native language skills as they learn to deal competently with English.

called on for their strengths as the teacher guides students through integrated and more meaningful language arts activities.

The fourth advantage of the extended-block schedule for the secondary English teacher is that it encourages the planning of meaningful and integrated activities more likely to repeatedly encompass the newly released *Standards for English Language Arts,* published jointly by the International Reading Association and the National Council of Teachers of English in 1996. The *Standards* urge us to nurture the ability to use language effectively and to encourage students to participate as knowledgeable and reflective participants.

Implementing the extended-block schedule provides an excellent time for us to analyze the integrated approach to teaching language studies. In one period, we can focus on a literary work while structuring activities to examine the structure of language and its conventions and also explore writing process applications related to the chosen text. The student can develop his or her skills in persuasion and research or compare and contrast cultural reactions to the text. The class period might include the elements shown in Figure 6–1, based on one literary work.

The language arts standards have been created in order to promote the goals described in Table 6–3 and to emphasize the components of language study outlined in Table 6–4.

The creators of the standards propose that students must develop the ability to utilize language in a variety of ways. They outline the purposes for developing competencies in English language arts as fourfold:

- For Obtaining and Communicating Information
- For Literary Response and Expression
- For Learning and Reflection
- For Problem Solving and Application (pp. 17–18)

The National Standards Committee emphasizes the necessity for integrated language experiences, stating:

> *We believe that students will best develop their knowledge, skills, and competencies through meaningful experiences and instruction that recognize purpose, form, and content as inextricably interrelated. (p. 14)*

FIGURE 6–1   Integrating the Standards in a 90-Minute Block: Five Activities

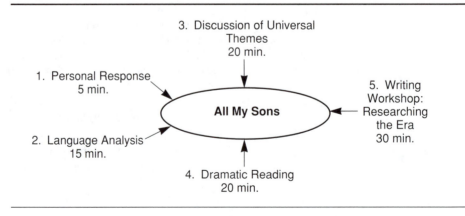

TABLE 6–3   The Goals of the Standards for the Language Arts

- To prepare students for the literacy demands of today and tomorrow
- To present a shared vision of literacy education
- To promote equity and excellence for all
- The standards reinforce the need for learning in the area of language arts to be an integrated process that utilizes the points listed in Table 6–4.

TABLE 6–4   Emphasized Components of Language Study

- A wide selection of literary, popular press, textbooks, and student-created works and the features of each
- The comprehension and application of a variety of processes and strategies through which students can develop competencies in language arts
- The knowledge of and competency in the systems, structure, and conventions of language as well as the application of this knowledge to various language tasks which address a variety of variables including audience

PLANNING INSTRUCTION FOR THE EXTENDED BLOCK

In contemplating instruction in the extended block, we recognize the need to reflect, either alone or with department colleagues and students, on the degree of student development in the language arts to be facilitated during this school year. From these established goals, we can then select the content most appropriate to each. For the four areas of reading, writing, speaking, and listening, the teacher needs to decide on the emphasis for each and to map out the approximate percentage of time within the 90 days of class meetings that will be devoted to student development in each. If, for example, the student should comprehend the struggles of the twentieth-century American in dealing with the complexity of technology and society's emphasis on materialism, the teacher may choose to study one literary work in depth instead of trying to cover the various selections that a thematically organized literary anthology might present. For general guidance on planning, see Figure 6–2, as well as Table 6–14 at the end of this chapter.

It becomes quickly apparent that a single activity, such as a lecture, a guided discussion, or a writer workshop session covering 90 minutes instead of the traditional 45- to 50-minute time frame will be unsuitable. Of the 90 minutes, the first 5 and the last 5 should be reserved for crucial introductions and wrap-ups. The remaining 80 minutes can then be divided into a variety of segment lengths according to the emphasis that the teacher has determined most beneficial to the students. However, a generalization about attention span also indicates that activities lasting longer than 20 minutes need internal refocusers to maintain student concentration. Planning a variety of activities aids the teacher in providing a productive 90 minutes as well. Generally, the outline depicted in Table 6–5 may be useful as a starting point.

Once you have determined which goals will be developed by this plan and you have begun to judge the number of appropriate activities to promote the greatest progress for each student, you can then work within the time frame by utilizing a number of teaching strategies and resources to address the needs of your students.

For example, a four-activity plan with a literary focus follows. Although the greatest amount of class time will be devoted to a specific literary assignment, this

FIGURE 6–2   **Planning in Chunks of Time: Building an Integrated English Plan**

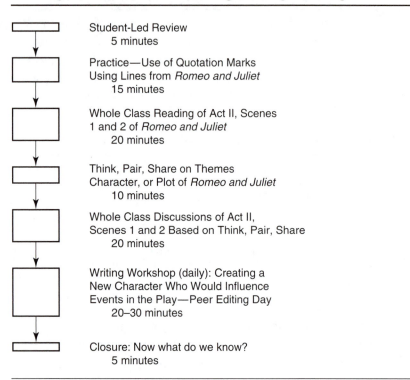

Student-Led Review
5 minutes

Practice—Use of Quotation Marks
Using Lines from *Romeo and Juliet*
15 minutes

Whole Class Reading of Act II, Scenes
1 and 2 of *Romeo and Juliet*
20 minutes

Think, Pair, Share on Themes
Character, or Plot of *Romeo and Juliet*
10 minutes

Whole Class Discussions of Act II,
Scenes 1 and 2 Based on Think, Pair, Share
20 minutes

Writing Workshop (daily): Creating a
New Character Who Would Influence
Events in the Play—Peer Editing Day
20–30 minutes

Closure: Now what do we know?
5 minutes

plan also incorporates the following in a 90-minute time frame: two related writing directives, practice in group consensus building, utilization of student-generated questions, linkage between student life experience and the universal theme of the literary piece, and a formal analysis of the structure of the English language. This plan contains traditional approaches to the teaching of literature. However, it changes the normal teacher-centered discussion by asking the students to generate pertinent questions on the text for use in whole-group discussion. By starting with student-generated questions, the teacher encourages a process through which stu-

TABLE 6–5   **General Lesson Plan Format**

Goals	Reading, Writing, Listening, Speaking
Standards Addressed	Next to each area below, list type of activity such as mini-lecture, cooperative learning, guided discussion, writing workshop session, journal entry, homework review, etc. Give a one- or two-sentence description of each activity and the approximate time for completion.
Activity 1:	Time: _____
Activity 2:	Time: _____
Activity 3:	Time: _____
Activity 4:	Time: _____
Activity 5:	Time: _____
Resources Needed	You might want to list handouts, overhead transparencies, news articles, anthology selections, rubrics, etc.

dents reflect more deeply on the literary piece and assume ownership of their learning. The questions that they create help them in the process of discovering meaning and comparing their interpretations with those of their peers. This series of activities promotes a pervasive theme in the reform movement. Langer (1992) notes that throughout the various aspects of educational reform, "one central theme has been the need to develop students' thinking abilities—the complex ways of approaching issues that underlie disciplined and reasoned thought" (p. 35).

COOPERATIVE LEARNING AND COLLABORATION: INTEGRAL COMPONENTS IN THE INTEGRATED LANGUAGE ARTS LESSON

As Table 6–6 indicates, formal cooperative learning configurations as well as informal collaborative strategies help the teacher to create a productive, student-centered environment. The modified Co-op, Co-op activity (see Kagan, 1985) requires small groups of students to produce a single product on which they all agree: a series of factual, inference, and prediction questions based on a specific literary work. This approach puts the burden of exploration on the students as they determine important questions to be asked and work together to communicate to each other the significance of their inquiry. Using this approach allows the teacher then to work in whole-group discussion with questions already created by the students instead of relying on a teacher-guided strategy, which traditionally leads the students to believe that only the teacher's questions and standard interpretations have value.

The simplest, yet consistently effective cooperative learning configurations applicable to the English classroom are also used in the integrated lesson depicted in Table 6–6. The students first reflect on the teacher-generated question in Activity 3

TABLE 6–6   An Integrated Four-Activity Plan: Literary Emphasis

Introductory Question/ Answer Session	This session links the previous day's lesson to today's.	5 minutes
Activity 1: Cooperative Learning Activity for Groups	Students generate five factual, five experience-based, and five inference or prediction questions on an assigned literary piece.	20 minutes
Activity 2: Whole-Class Discussion	Student-generated questions are used to explore the work.	20 minutes
Activity 3: Individual Student Writing	Students respond to a crucial teacher-designed question linking an important theme in the piece to personal experience, and share the response.	20 minutes
Activity 4: Analysis of Language Use	The teacher and students analyze a teacher-selected or student-selected passage to discover the structure and conventions of the language that effectively convey an important impression or mood.	20 minutes
Wrap-up: A Quick Write	What did you learn today, and what questions remain in your mind?	5 minutes

and respond in a journal entry; they then pair with a partner to compare responses. Finally, they share with the class their individual interpretations and experiential applications. Think (or Write)-Pair-Share can be utilized repeatedly to encourage deeper student reflection and student exposure to the interpretations of their peers and adults.

As outlined in Chapter 3, the Jigsaw configuration is particularly useful when the teacher wishes to reinforce large chunks of material in a quicker yet more concentrated manner. For example, the teacher can structure a Jigsaw activity to review sentence types, comma placement, quotation use, and effective modifiers by providing each base group with a lengthy passage from a current news article. That article might reflect an issue that is already the focus of a literary assignment. The base group then divides into expert groups in order to study the text for one of the four structural aspects mentioned above. After expert groups have analyzed the passage relative to their particular task, they return to their base groups in order to inform the other members of their knowledge. In subsequent class discussion, the teacher can add or clarify any of the structural aspects still in question. Students then return to their own writing better able to apply the structure of the language to their work in progress. In addition to reviewing structural aspects of the language, the Jigsaw is also useful for analysis and/or review of longer reading assignments.

The Roundrobin cooperative learning strategy is also particularly useful if the teacher wishes students to gain a deep understanding of point of view and of the reliable/unreliable narrator. After the teacher has explained first/third-limited/omniscient/stream-of-consciousness, for example, students may use a well-known tale to practice storytelling in various narrations. *The Tortoise and the Hare* can be re-created as one student writes the first sentence of the story and then hands it to the next member of the group to continue in whichever point of view he or she has

TABLE 6–7   An Integrated Language Arts Lesson Emphasizing Point of View

Activity 1	The teacher reads a short passage done in the omniscient point of view. The students then listen as he or she reads the same passage but in the first-person point of view. The teacher poses questions to the students so that they analyze the difference between the two passages. The teacher then gives the various points of view as a mini-lecture.	15 minutes
Activity 2	Using the Roundrobin and a tale supplied by the teacher, students re-create a folktale utilizing a new point of view. Groups are assigned various points of view. Groups share their re-creations with the class.	20 minutes
Activity 3	The teacher and students look at two examples of unreliable narrators and discuss the technique of using an unreliable narrator.	15 minutes
Activity 4	Roundrobin groups convene to re-create *Jack and the Beanstalk* with the Giant as the unreliable narrator. Groups share re-creations.	20 minutes
Activity 5	Students individually pick a short passage and rewrite it as a journal entry.	15 minutes
Wrap-up	Volunteer students read their entries and the class guesses the point of view used.	5 minutes

been assigned. The same tale can be re-created once, twice, or multiple times using various points of view (see Table 6–7).

The concept of the reliable/unreliable narrator is also a difficult one for students to grasp. Once they compare with the teacher a passage from "The Tell Tale Heart" or, depending on the group, *The Sound and the Fury*, the concept of unreliable narrator is introduced. If they then use the Roundrobin to re-create *Jack and the Beanstalk*, with the Giant giving a purposely distorted account, the concept of unreliable narrator becomes much clearer. Next, the students go back to their journals, choose a short passage from the literary piece that they are currently reading, and rewrite that passage using another point of view. This series of activities provides the opportunity not only to learn about point of view and to analyze various points of view but also to manipulate narration and to experience a difficult literary concept on a much deeper level.

INQUIRY LEARNING AND THE INTEGRATED LANGUAGE ARTS LESSON

The English teacher can effectively blend the strengths of traditional strategies such as the mini-lecture, guided discussion, analysis of rhetorical structures, and argumentation with more contemporary strategies of reader response, cooperative learning, and process writing to give the students even more opportunity to examine the power of language and to use that power in their own lives. The inquiry-based learning cycle format described in Chapter 4 provides the structure to achieve these goals.

High school students, especially juniors and seniors, are in a crucial stage of development. They are moving from concrete operations to more abstract thinking and are capable of understanding concepts such as democracy, liberty, oppression, and discrimination, especially when grounded in concrete experience first. In addition, they are formulating their own personal concept of the individual's duties to society. (We have all experienced their willingness to point out to us our own behaviors and label us hypocrites!) Connecting with these developments, English teachers can incorporate into their literary curricula various examples of the literature of revolution and dissent. Related to this type of literary work, it is important for those of us teaching English to understand Adelson's theory of the development of a social ideology (1972):

> *For students who feel the oppression of rules and restrictions, who have the feeling that something is wrong and imbalanced in the world but do not have channels of response, reading such literature is a means for ordering their thoughts and understanding potentials and possibilities for action. (Smagorinsky, 1990, p. 15)*

Thus, selections like Patrick Henry's "Speech before the Virginia Convention—March 23, 1775" and Martin Luther King, Jr.'s, "I Have a Dream" can be used as the basis for an integrated learning experience based on the learning cycle structure described in Chapter 4. The following plan completes Phase One and Phase Two in the first 90-minute class session. Phase Three can be completed in part of the next class, or it can involve the next two or three classes, depending on the teacher's decision to use Phase Three for application of concepts learned in the first two phases or for expansion.

The teacher may feel that specific student needs in this class would be better served by following Phase Two with an expansion activity in the third phase of the

TABLE 6–8   An Integrated Approach to the Literature of Dissent

Activity 1	Phase One—Exploration—Individual Reading and Reader-Response Journal Entry: Students read Patrick Henry's speech silently and write their thoughts in their journals.	15 minutes
Activity 2	Heads Together Cooperative Learning: Students make hypotheses about the persuasive power of Henry's speech and what about it made his listeners enlist in his cause. They prepare textual references to support their hypotheses.	15 minutes
Activity 3	Phase Two—Invention Guided Discussion: Students reconvene for whole-group sharing of their hypotheses and supporting observations. The teacher lists pertinent information on the board.	20 minutes
Activity 4	Mini-lecture: Building on student input, the teacher gives new information on rhetorical structures: rhetorical questions, parallel structure, contrasting imagery, appeals to patriotism and God, etc.	20 minutes
Activity 5	Phase Three—Application or Expansion (Application): Students take the information learned from Phase I and Phase II, applying it to the analysis of Martin Luther King, Jr.'s "I Have a Dream."	(End Day 1 and using some of Day 2)
Activity 6	Students share their individual analysis with a partner and then with the class.	

learning cycle. An activity based on a social or historical perspective includes using the time-honored strategy of copying the orator's style while creating a speech or writing a passage on an issue of importance to the student writer. In addition, the teacher may see this series of activities as logical preparation for an expansion ac-

Students benefit from the time that allows them to move from concrete operations to abstract thinking.

tivity in which students write their own persuasive speeches using the rhetorical strategies of Patrick Henry, Martin Luther King, Jr., or any other of the famous writers of revolution and dissent. Such a third phase would involve the steps of process writing and the presentation of the persuasive speech to the class.

Thus, if the teacher determines application to be the better choice, the learning cycle could be completed in little over one class period. If expansion is selected, the amount of time will vary with the activity chosen. This format promotes the integration of the language arts. It presents language structure in meaningful context. It adds the student's personal beliefs to rhetorical argument, providing meaningful, retentive learning experiences for the language arts student as well as opportunities for the development of the adolescent's growing sense of his or her place in society.

INCORPORATING LEARNING STATIONS INTO LITERATURE, WRITING, AND GRAMMAR/USAGE INSTRUCTION

Teachers worry about not covering enough content if their classes are to be completed in one semester on the 4×4 block. If they are committed to the alternating-day extended schedule, they express concern about making in-depth assignments when students now have eight classes per school year instead of seven. Learning stations can constitute lessons in which students deal with content in depth within one class period.

For example, a literary text can be studied in depth by constructing a series of learning stations requiring students to apply the text to a number of contexts (see Table 6–9). The learning station plan contains variety and depth as well as opportunity for student choice. Milner and Milner (1993) employ the learning station format in the study of *Huckleberry Finn*. They suggest that students complete one station per day for six days. However, the extended-block period will allow two stations to be accomplished in one class period, so that students complete the learning stations in only three days. An advantage of using this learning station series within the extended block in three days is that the activities need not be interrupted by the weekend.

TABLE 6–9 Milner and Milner's Textual Learning Stations

1. River Chart
2. What if . . . Huck Finn
3. Jim's Diary
4. River Talk–Shore Speak
5. Women's Portraits
6. Scams
7. Artistocracy–Democracy
8. Mark Twain's Humor
9. The Newspaper
10. Religious Professions

TABLE 6–10 Learning Stations in the Extended-Block Period: Innocence to Experience

Activity 1	*Introductory Journal Entry:* Students respond to the teacher's question: *Huckleberry Finn* has been described as a journey from innocence to experience. Defend this statement giving examples from the text.	10 minutes
Activity 2	All students must complete Learning Station #1: River Chart.	30 minutes
Activity 3	Students choose one of the nine remaining stations. They may work individually or in pairs depending on the assignment of the station chosen.	30 minutes
Activity 4	*Whole-group Discussion:* At this time, the teacher returns to the journal entry, guiding students through the universal theme of a person's journey from innocence to experience.	10 minutes
Activity 5	*Wrap-up*: The teacher questions the students about other previously assigned texts dealing with the same theme.	5 minutes
Assignment	Students finish remaining work on their chosen learning stations for Day 1; students complete a journal entry drawing parallels between the innocence to experience theme in *Huckleberry Finn* and the same theme in other texts which they have named in the Wrap Up.	

Among the stations are assignments that ask the students to map the route taken by Huck, predict the consequences for Huck and Jim of alternative story lines, write about the unfolding events through Jim's eyes as they create Jim's diary, and study the dialect as well as the imagery contained in language.

Such a list of learning stations provides choice for the students and yet demands ample textual investigation for class discussion. In 90 minutes, the teacher can direct the students to complete two learning stations and still bring the class together to emphasize other aspects of the novel. Table 6–10 provides a sample learning station plan for one extended-block period based on the theme of moving from innocence to experience.

This plan integrates writing, reading, speaking, and listening skills. It makes use of activities which appeal to various learning styles.

To create a series of learning stations that investigate an important literary topic, Milner and Milner (1993) suggest that teachers construct five learning stations with the provision that students need to complete four of the five stations. Milner and Milner's topical stations can form the basis of a learning station lesson that reinforces the recurring literary theme of the search for the American Dream. The teacher creates five stations that engage the students in deep learning about the concept. Table 6–11 illustrates five possibilities for investigation.

Learning stations also provide a convenient format for dealing with student errors in writing. Students take more seriously discussions of sentence errors, punctuation, and usage when those problems are surfacing in their writing workshop drafts. The teacher can make use of this heightened interest by using students' own writing samples to create a series of learning stations focusing on correct grammatical structures, mechanics, and usage. Preparation for this series of learning stations can be initiated by analysis of student errors. The use of a student tally grid that contains the most often repeated errors makes such analysis simple. When the students are at the final revision stage of a baseline writing sample, they confer with the teacher and then chart in their writing errors. When the draft is then rewritten

TABLE 6–11 Topical Learning Stations: The American Dream

Station 1	List five accomplishments you hope to attain in your life. With your group members, compare lists; under your own list, write a paragraph in which you compare the similarities and differences among your group members in describing their personal American Dream.
Station 2	Construct a debate on (1) civic and social responsibility versus individual rights as they relate to the pursuit of the American Dream or (2) the possibility of attaining the American Dream in today's world. The debate will be presented on a date to be announced.
Station 3	Apply the concept of the American Dream as including material wealth, civil and religious freedom, and opportunity, to two characters in *My Antonia* by Willa Cather. Make a chart with the dreams of both, their experiences, and an estimation of their struggle to attain the American Dream. Create a new event in which one of the characters makes a decision that changes the development of events in the novel. Write the description of the event, the decision, and the results of that decision for the course of the story. Complete this assignment in a Roundrobin writing format with the members of your group.
Station 4	Using *The Great Gatsby* by F. Scott Fitzgerald, draw two pictures. The first will depict Gatsby surrounded by his concept of the American Dream; the second will depict you in a setting that visually describes your personal American Dream. Prepare the two drawings for class display. Be prepared to explain the drawings and the depiction of the American Dream in each.
Station 5	At this station are four prints of famous paintings. Study all four. Decide the manner in which the American Dream is depicted in each. Make a group decision on the painting that best agrees with your concept of the American Dream. Present your group's choice and rationale in our debriefing session. The paintings are as follows: West's *Penn Treaty with the Indians,* Hicks's *The Peaceable Kingdom,* Doughty's *In Nature's Wonderland,* and Cole's *The Voyage of Life: Youth.* If none of the prints approximates the group's concept of the American Dream, the group is to identify elements in each that do relate to their concept or to use library resources and/or electronic access to American art museums in order to locate a more appropriate example done by an American artist to present to the class.

as the final piece and evaluated by the teacher, the student returns to the tally grid, indicating whether or not the problem area has been successfully eliminated (see Table 6–12).

After the student has completed at least two writing assignments and filled in the individual chart, the teacher can collect the charts and quickly analyze areas for reinforcement. Those areas become the focus of the personalized and contextualized learning stations.

Depending on the number of stations constructed for a particular session, each student or group of students may choose four or five for one day's work. After explaining the stations, the teacher distributes Station Completion Sheets to each group. They consult their individual tally sheets to determine which stations will address their errors, thus benefitting them most. Table 6–13 gives an example of four possible learning stations based on students and their own writing.

After students have completed the learning stations, the teacher conducts a debriefing session, showing the students examples from their own writing in order to

TABLE 6–12   Student Tally Grid: Sheet 1

Student Tally Grid						
NAME—CLASS SECTION	SAMPLE—DATE	(+) (–)	SAMPLE 1—DATE	(+) (–1)	SAMPLE 2—DATE	(+) (–)
RANDOLF, JASON PERIOD 2	BASELINE—9/13		2/20/97			
AREAS OF CONCERN						
SENTENCE FRAGMENTS						
RUN-ON SENTENCES						
SUBJECT–VERB	/ /	(–)	/ /	(+)		
VERB FORMS	/ / /	(–)	/	(+)		
PRONOUN–ANTECEDENT	/ /	(+)	/ /	(+)		
COMMA WITH INTRODUCTORY PHRASES/CLAUSES	/	(+)	/ / /	(+)		
COMMA IN COMPOUND SENTENCE	/	(+)				
COMMAS—OTHER (LIST BELOW)						
COMMA, SERIES	/	(+)				
COMMA, DIRECT ADDRESS	/	(+)	/	(+)		
APOSTROPHE USE	/ /	(–)	/ / /	(–)		
HOMONYMS (LIST BELOW)						
SIGHT, CITE, SITE	/	(+)				
THERE, THEIR, THEY'RE	/	(+)	/ /			
SPELLING (LIST)						
OTHER						

Source: From "Writing Projects: Taking Teachers through the Looking Glass" by M. Bevevino, edited by E. L. Thompson, *Virginia English Bulletin,* Vol. 47, No. 2, Fall 1997. Used with permission of the *Virginia English Bulletin.*

review the concepts covered in the learning stations. Periodically, as the students participate in the writing workshop, they will fill in the tally grid. The teacher can then construct a series of learning stations at a future date so that the most common errors in writing are addressed.

As English teachers, we now have the opportunity to use our expertise and to focus our concern for the ability of students to gain power from the use of their language by planning sustained sessions which incorporate reading, writing, listening, and speaking in meaningful ways. The extended-block schedule can breathe new life into the secondary English curriculum and give renewed hope to teachers whose goal is to produce young people who will be enriched and empowered by their proficiency in their language.

TABLE 6–13 Dealing with Student Error through Learning Stations

Station 1	Subject–Verb Agreement/Correct Verb Forms Students read a two-page story, a humorous narrative about the class itself, utilizing student names. They list all subject–verb combinations, correcting agreement or verb form errors, and self-correcting their work with an answer key.
Station 2	Pronoun–Antecedent Agreement Students are asked to pick two sentences from their own writing portfolios and revise according to the station's directions. Students self-correct using the provided list of possible pronoun–antecedent combinations listed at the station.
Station 3	Verb Forms Students use a series of 10 pictures to create pairs of sentences for 8 of the pictures. They must begin the first sentence with "Yesterday," and the second must contain *have, has,* or *had* with another verb form. Sentences are left at the station for subsequent teacher correction.
Station 4	Phrases and Clauses with Comma Use Students manipulate strips containing phrases and clauses to create various sentences. The strips are based on sample sentences that the teacher has taken from student writing. Markers for capital letters and commas are provided. Students put sentences together as directed and place markers in appropriate places. Self-correcting answer keys are provided.

TABLE 6–14 Putting Your Thoughts in Order: English

1. List the most important concepts/skills that you want your students to understand/master before they walk out of your room at the end of the course.
2. List content selections to address each goal.
3. List effective activities now used to address each goal.
4. Indicate which concepts/skills you wish to address in more depth.
5. Think of ways in which you can personalize or contextualize each goal.
6. Consider various strategies that you might add to address each goal: cooperative learning, inquiry learning, study skill strategies. List them for each goal.

Goals	1. Concept Skills	2. Content Selections	3. Current Activities	4. More Depth	5. Personalize, Contextualize	6. New Ideas
1.						
2.						
3.						
4.						
5.						
6.						
7.						
8.						
9.						
10.						

■ 7
Teaching Science

SCIENCE TEACHERS WHO have been blessed with one laboratory period per week under traditional class scheduling know of the benefits of a double lab period. This chapter will examine the advantages inherent in the traditional science laboratory as well as several other potential advantages in science education that extended-block scheduling affords teachers and students.

ADVANTAGES IN THE SCIENCE CLASSROOM

There are at least seven distinct advantages to block scheduling for science teachers:

1. The reduction in demands placed on physical space and science equipment necessary for a well-designed laboratory experience is an important advantage science teachers using block scheduling are quick to point out. Instead of 150 or more students moving through a traditional laboratory experience each day, attempting to set up, conduct, and clean up the lab in 45 minutes, 75 students engage in the laboratory in 90-minute blocks of time. This reduced class size increases the safety of the science laboratory and reduces the amount of time spent setting up and cleaning up. It is not uncommon to conduct, within one 90-minute block, a traditional laboratory that would have taken three 45-minute class periods over three consecutive days.

2. The flexibility of block scheduling allows science teachers to schedule labs on any given day of the week, not just the single day on which a double period may have been provided. Students are given more opportunity to complete a laboratory experience, including data organization, data analysis, and formation of conclusions, before hurrying off to the next class.

3. Extended-block scheduling provides an increased opportunity to engage in discovery-oriented science (see Chapter 4). Although traditional (verification) laboratory experiences are necessary in every science discipline, discovery laboratory experiences as delivered via learning cycle and inquiry approaches truly engage the learner as a scientist. Learning cycle and inquiry methods can be maximized under the extended-block schedule. Examples of each are included later in this chapter.

4. The full development of mathematical relationships inherent in the important scientific principles to be learned in every secondary science classroom is best accomplished by using a gradual progression from concrete to abstract understanding. Given more time each day, teachers and students can collectively uncover the meaning behind various formulae instead of simply memorizing the formula and proceeding with "mindless application"—problem-solving drill and practice exercises.

5. The extended block provides ample time to examine laboratory data by using simple descriptive and inferential statistical analysis. For example, students take raw data and enter it into a spreadsheet. Graphic representations of data are generated and may be interpreted. Relationships and cause–effect can be explored by using simple correlational and inferential statistical tools.

6. Teacher demonstrations can be followed by a more in-depth inquiry with students if one has a 90-minute time block. Instead of developing the important concepts demonstrated on the following day, the discussion may be completed while the demonstration is still fresh in the minds of the students.

7. The extended block may provide more opportunity for students to connect science, technology, and relevant social issues. In order for students to see the importance of science and its role in their daily lives, opportunities must be provided for them to investigate science-related social issues.

SCIENCE EDUCATION REFORM AND SCIENCE STANDARDS

Taking advantage of intensive scheduling requires a shift from traditional science teaching that has allowed science teachers to cover more topics, but that leaves students with a smattering of isolated facts, concepts, and vocabulary.

> *Teachers have relied heavily on textbooks and lectures to convey large quantities of information, and students have been expected to memorize reams of facts and terminology. Hands-on experiences have been limited to "cookbook labs" with outcomes known in advance, not real investigations. In most classrooms, science has been presented as an inert body of knowledge to be assimilated, rather than a process of inquiry and a way to make sense of our world. (Willis, 1995, p. 1)*

Drawing on prior knowledge, students attack a new concept, hypothesizing and predicting the sequence of steps needed to solve the teacher-posed question.

In science classrooms where "telling" is the predominant form of instruction, students sit and listen or read about science. They may even learn the "rules of the game"—the scientific method—by rote. But they rarely if ever "get into the game" and act as scientists. Major organizations in the science education community—the National Science Foundation (NSF), the National Science Teachers Association (NSTA), and the American Association for the Advancement of Science (AAAS)—are vigorously promoting hands-on, inquiry-based activities (Willis, 1995).

The science education reform themes include the following:

1. Learning concepts is more important than memorizing of facts and terms.
2. Students should have ample opportunities for hands-on learning. Concrete experiences with actual phenomena should precede more abstract lessons.
3. Science instruction should be inquiry-based, at least in part. Students should have opportunities to pose their own questions, design and pursue their own investigations, analyze data, and present their findings.
4. Teachers should teach fewer concepts, in greater depth, rather than covering a great many topics superficially. (Less is more.)

Both *Project 2061: Science for All Americans* (AAAS) and *Scope, Sequence and Coordination of Secondary School Science* (NSTA) embrace these general guidelines.

The standards established by each of the science education reform reports encompass five major goals for science education (Table 7–1). These goals can be viewed as curriculum guides that can ensure a balanced approach to science education.

One coherent perspective on what scientific literacy embraces is offered by the National Science Education Standards (1995). Eight categories of content standards were developed, and conceptual frameworks were identified within each. The eight categories are as follows: (1) Unifying Concepts and Processes, (2) Science as Inquiry, (3) Physical Science, (4) Life Science, (5) Earth and Space Science, (6) Science and Technology, (7) Science in Personal and Social Perspectives, and (8) History and Nature of Science.

TABLE 7–1   Five Major Goals for Science Education

1. Scientific Knowledge	Science education should develop a fundamental understanding of natural systems.
2. Scientific Method	Science education should develop a fundamental understanding of, and ability to use, the methods of scientific investigation.
3. Societal Issues	Science education should prepare citizens to make responsible decisions concerning science-related social issues.
4. Personal Needs	Science education should contribute to an understanding and fulfillment of personal needs, thereby contributing to personal development.
5. Career Awareness	Science education should inform students about careers in the sciences.

Historically, science education in the United States has been driven by scientific knowledge, to the near exclusion of the other four overarching goals. Although several model curricula were developed in the post-Sputnik era, many were abandoned because of lack of financial support, followed by a return to content-driven models. Lost in the back-to-basics, content-driven, coverage models was the opportunity for students to learn and use science process skills—to act as scientists. The current consensus for reform coupled with the implementation of intensive scheduling opens the way for exciting opportunities for students to learn science "as scientists" and to develop critical science process skills. Table 7–2 lists 13 key science process skills.

These skills should not be taught in isolation, devoid of any scientific conceptual framework. Rather, as students engage in meaningful lessons, designed to focus on fewer concepts in more depth, part of their science experience will allow them to use a variety of these process skills in conjunction with the science content.

TABLE 7–2   Thirteen Science Process Skills

1. *Defining Problems:* It is important to clarify questions we wish to answer through scientific inquiry.

2. *Designing Investigations:* It is important to plan a scientific investigation carefully, considering variables and potential difficulties.

3. *Conducting Controlled Experiments:* The thinking process involved here attempts to control all the factors except the variable being tested by the researcher.

4. *Observing:* Most science inquiry involves observing, often with several senses, and requires care and objectivity.

5. *Measuring:* Measurement of scientific phenomena includes appropriate selection and use of tools and instruments, precision, and sources of error.

6. *Classifying:* The assembly of groups of objects, observations, events, or conditions of an investigation based on shared characteristics is useful in scientific inquiry.

7. *Inferring:* Students need to see the difference between inference and observation, and to recognize when they use inference to move beyond data that have been collected.

8. *Formulating Hypotheses:* These are mental constructs that serve as suggested or anticipated answers (predictions). Hypotheses creatively drive the investigation.

9. *Collecting and Handling Data:* The construction of tables, diagrams, graphs, and other visual organizers takes students beyond raw data to organized formats.

10. *Interpreting Data:* Graphic representations may permit the student to identify patterns in data; and simple statistical tools, both descriptive and inferential, can allow students to quantify relationships and causality.

11. *Searching Literature:* Scientific inquiry should not occur in isolation, independent of other resources that can lead to an understanding of natural systems and phenomena.

12. *Relating to Theory:* The scientific inquiry should not simply become a technical exercise. Rather, it should relate to broad scientific constructs that unify the scientific knowledge base.

13. *Drawing Conclusions:* Students need to know when to suspend judgment, offer tentative conclusions, and defend their conclusions based on empirical evidence from the inquiry. They should be willing to take intellectual risks in the science classroom.

PLANNING FOR SCIENCE INSTRUCTION

Consider the following scenario: A biology teacher contemplates the school district's move to semester block scheduling. Given the freedom to adapt to the new schedule, he or she decides to change nothing. The students will be meeting for the same number of class hours; therefore, they will receive two 45-minute lectures in one 90-minute block. Planning completed.

In this classroom, teaching and learning are perceived as telling and listening. The temptation simply to talk twice as much ignores the reform recommendations and puts students into a passive, nonconstructivist mode for up to 90 minutes. Perhaps the teacher will allow them to begin homework during the last 15 minutes of class to "break up the monotony." Such simplistic, narrow views of block scheduling never take advantage of the time made available. Greater flexibility in planning should be seen as an opportunity to experiment, collect empirical evidence on the impact of the new plan, and revise to meet the needs of the students. For more guidance on planning, see Figure 7–1 below and Table 7–11 at the end of the chapter (page 94).

The Traditional Laboratory Revisited

Verification labs are typically found in the laboratory manuals that accompany the course text. The students essentially act as technicians, following directions listed in the procedure, collecting data, and/or answering questions in some format or other (see Table 7–3). These lab experiences are valuable and necessary for three

FIGURE 7–1   Planning in Chunks of Time: Building an Integrated Science Plan

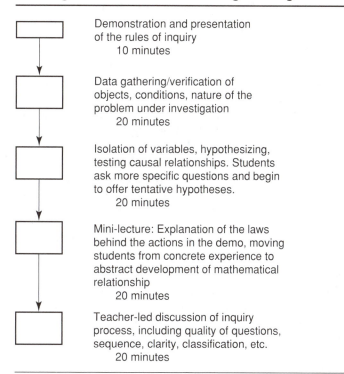

Demonstration and presentation
of the rules of inquiry
10 minutes

Data gathering/verification of
objects, conditions, nature of the
problem under investigation
20 minutes

Isolation of variables, hypothesizing,
testing causal relationships. Students
ask more specific questions and begin
to offer tentative hypotheses.
20 minutes

Mini-lecture: Explanation of the laws
behind the actions in the demo, moving
students from concrete experience to
abstract development of mathematical
relationship
20 minutes

Teacher-led discussion of inquiry
process, including quality of questions,
sequence, clarity, classification, etc.
20 minutes

TABLE 7–3 **Verification Lab General Lesson Format**

Process Skills: (List)

Standards Addressed: (check) SK ✔ SM ✔ CA___ SI___ PN___

Activity		Time
Activity 1	Procedural overview/safety considerations	
Activity 2	Conduct verification lab	
Activity 3	Clean up	
Activity 4	Data organization/analysis	
Activity 5	Presentation/comparison of findings	
Activity 6	Difficulties/sources of error/other	

reasons. First, they allow students to practice techniques with equipment that may be new to them. Second, students may need very structured experiences to learn to use materials and equipment safely. Third, the lab may lead into a discovery-oriented experience that will follow this common classroom experience. As mentioned earlier in this chapter, the extended-block schedule maximizes the laboratory time. In planning for these "cookbook" laboratory experiences, consider the format shown in Table 7–3.

Most of the time spent in the verification laboratory is usually within Activity 2, the actual laboratory investigation. Depending on the complexity of the lab and the type of data collected (quantitative or qualitative), the application of data analysis will vary. Asking students why the procedure was established as it was in a verification laboratory can reveal their understanding of the process involved in the investigation. The lab becomes more than a "follow the directions" exercise.

Inquiry Planning

Two methods of science inquiry, BSCS Inquiry and the Inquiry Training Model, were presented in Chapter 4. Examples are provided here in specific science content areas to serve as planning templates for each inquiry method. Remember, inquiry differs from verification learning experiences because the learner has not already been taught the correct answer or outcome. Table 7–4 shows how the BSCS Inquiry Model is used in a seed germination experiment.

As part of Schwab's "Invitations to Enquiry" in *Biological Sciences Curriculum Study* (1965), this BSCS Inquiry model asks students to investigate problems as a research biologist. Students might work independently with the data set and description of the experiment on seed germination, or they can work in research teams. Once the students have reviewed the "invitation," the teacher requires that the students defend their interpretations of the data. Students are then required to do a critical analysis of the experiment as designed, isolate problems or flaws, state the main problem with the investigation, and move toward rectifying the errors by redesigning the investigation. They are encouraged to share these new designs at the end of the class meeting. Individually or as teams, students should defend their designs and be open to constructive criticism. This could be followed by a discovery laboratory the next day in which lab teams follow their own designs. Notice how the students are directly engaged in the development of the process skills of defining problems, designing experiments, inferring, and interpreting data.

TABLE 7–4   BSCS Inquiry Model: Life Science—Seed Germination

Process Skills: (List) Defining Problems, Designing Experiments, Inferring, Interpreting Data

Standards Addressed: (check) SK ✔   SM ✔   CA___   SI___   PN___

Activity		Time
Activity 1	Overview of lesson provided for students	5 minutes
Activity 2	Phase One—Area of Investigation is posed to the student. Teacher presents students with a scenario in which an investigator attempts to determine the best conditions for seed germination. Experimental design errors are included in the scenario.	15 minutes
Activity 3	Phase Two—Students structure the problem. Students are asked to interpret the data on the basis of evidence from the experiment alone. The discussion focuses on the teacher challenging students' thinking and sources of evidence. Students begin to rethink the problem under investigation and to develop a clear problem statement.	20 minutes
Activity 4	Phase Three—Students identify the problem in the investigation, design errors made.	15 minutes
Activity 5	Phase Four—Students redesign the experiment.	20 minutes
Activity 6	Students present/defend ideas for new experimental designs.	15 minutes

The next lesson sample is drawn from physical science, as an example of the five-phase Inquiry Training Model applied to Newton's Laws (Table 7–5).

The physics student is confronted with a demonstration using two small boats, identical in construction except for the position of a small battery-operated fan. On one boat, the fan, mounted to the deck of the boat, pushes air into the sail. On the other boat, the fan is turned 180 degrees and is pushing air behind the boat. Students must engage in the questioning process of this inquiry model (see Chapter 4) in order to determine why the boats behave differently. The time frames indicated here are approximate. Since this lesson is student driven, the teacher may accelerate a class by giving clues if the line of questioning gets off target. The content is not taught until a correct hypothesis is offered and can be defended by the class. The students begin with a concrete experience and move through data collection by questioning, and ultimately the teacher provides direct instruction on the concept during Phase Four. The students finish the lesson by analyzing the process of inquiry. In this 90-minute inquiry lesson, the science process skills of defining problems, observing, inferring, formulating hypotheses, collecting and handling data, and interpreting data have been practiced in conjunction with a physical science concept.

Planning the Learning Cycle

The extended-block schedule is ideally suited for learning cycle instruction in science. Like most valuable verification laboratories, the learning cycle requires more than the traditional 45 minutes to complete. Many science learning cycle experiences can be completed within a single 90-minute period. The examples provided

TABLE 7–5 **Inquiry Training Model: Newton's Laws**

Process Skills: (List) Defining Problems, Observing, Inferring, Formulating Hypotheses, Collecting and Handling Data, Interpreting Data

Standards Addressed: (check) SK **✔** SM **✔** CA___ SI___ PN___

Activity		Time
Activity 1	Phase One—Confrontation with the problem. Students are presented with demonstration of two sailing ship models, and the rules of inquiry.	10 minutes
Activity 2	Phase Two—Data gathering, verification. Students ask yes/no questions designed to verify the nature of the objects in the discrepant event, conditions in the demonstration, and the nature of the problem under investigation.	20 minutes
Activity 3	Phase Three—Isolate variables, hypothesize and test causal relationships. Students continue to ask more specific questions; begin to offer tentative hypotheses.	20 minutes
Activity 4	Phase Four—Formulation of rules, explanation. Teacher explains the law behind the different actions of each of the two ships. Begins to move students from concrete experience to abstract development of mathematical relationship.	20 minutes
Activity 5	Phase Five—Analysis of inquiry strategies used. Teacher-led discussion of inquiry process used. Quality of questions, sequence, clarity, classification of questions, etc.	20 minutes

are taken from physics, chemistry, and biology. They illustrate the three-phase approach described in Chapter 3. Table 7–6 shows the use of the learning cycle to study the pendulum.

In this learning cycle, the students follow a brief teacher-directed demonstration of a simple pendulum. They are expected to record, *in their own words,* what they observe. Students are then asked to list the measurements that could be made. Finally, they are asked to list changes that could be made. Observations, measurements, and changes are shared with the class. The teacher keeps a list of the student language used in Phase One.

Phase Two begins with the teacher pointing to accurate, relevant observations and assigning the correct scientific language to each. This is repeated for measurement and for the variables suggested. For example, a student watches the pendulum and observes that "it goes back and forth in a rhythm." The teacher links this student language to the cycle or harmonic motion of the pendulum. A student suggests that the length of the string could be changed. The teacher refers to this as a change in the radius length or arm of the pendulum.

Once all terminology has been related to the student language, students are asked to predict the effect of changing one variable on the period of the pendulum. Once the predictions are made, lab teams are assigned a variable and a procedure. Data are collected and analyzed, and conclusions are tentatively drawn by each team. Finally, each team reports their data and findings. Discrepancies are discussed and sources of error are exposed.

Table 7–7 illustrates the application of a learning cycle to the understanding of rates of chemical reactions. Notice that in this learning cycle, during the Phase One

TABLE 7–6   Physics Learning Cycle: The Pendulum

Process Skills: (List)

Standards Addressed: (check) SK ✔ SM ✔ CA___ SI___ PN___

Activity		Time
Activity 1	Phase One—Exploration Students observe a teacher demonstration of a simple pendulum. Key questions: What do you observe? What can we measure? What could we change?	10 minutes
Activity 2	Phase Two—Concept Invention Students share observations, ideas for measurement, variable possibilities.	20 minutes
Activity 3	Phase Two—Concept Invention Teacher uses student responses, links student language to scientific language [*mass, radius, displacement, period, cycle*].	20 minutes
Activity 4	Phase Three—Discovery/Application Teacher assigns one variable to each lab team. Students determine the relationship between mass, displacement, radius, and period in lab setting.	25 minutes
Activity 5	Presentation of Data—Student lab teams share data, draw conclusions.	15 minutes

TABLE 7–7   Chemistry Learning Cycle: Rates of Chemical Reactions

Process Skills: (List)

Standards Addressed: (check) SK ✔ SM ✔ CA___ SI___ PN___

Activity		Time
Activity 1	Phase One—Exploration Students complete a verification lab using two reactants to form a single solid product at room temperature. They measure the mass of the precipitate and record all data.	25 minutes
Activity 2	Phase Two—Concept Invention Students share observations. Teacher invents from student language the concept of rate of reaction, and asks students to suggest conditions that could affect the rate of a chemical reaction.	10 minutes
Activity 3	Phase Two—Concept Invention The teacher asks students to hypothesize the effect of each variable and narrows the list of variables to pH and temperature.	10 minutes
Activity 4	Phase Three—Discovery/Application Lab teams design experiments to test their hypotheses. Lab designs must be approved by the teacher before they begin their experimentation.	15 minutes
Activity 5	Phase Three—Discovery/Application Lab teams follow their lab designs and conduct the inquiry.	25 minutes

exploration, students engage in a structured verification laboratory that allows them to practice technique and data collection process skills. During Phase Two, the teacher invents the key concept of reaction rate and asks students to identify variables that may affect the rate of a given chemical reaction. From the list of suggestions, the teacher assigns teams to investigate the effect of reactant temperature of pH of solution on reaction rates. Instead of providing each team with a procedure as in the previous learning cycle, lab teams must design the experiment, submit it for approval, and then move to the lab bench to perform the experiment during Phase Three.

During the following class meeting, lab teams either finish conducting the lab or, if finished, prepare to present their findings and tentative conclusions. Because several teams are investigating the same variable, but following different lab designs, they can engage in constructive criticism of each others work. Lab team members should be able to defend their procedure and lab design, or acknowledge flaws that emanate from this peer review.

The final example of a learning cycle and its utility within the extended block of 90 minutes is applied to the life science concept of osmosis (Table 7–8). Instead of simply teaching students the principle via diagram or lecture, the teacher exposes them to the concept first through a teacher-designed lab station. The students observe, record what they observe in their own words, and list what they can measure. They are asked to explain what they think is causing the "CELL" (dialysis tubing bag) to appear normal in one container, but shrunken in another.

In Phase Two, they share observations, what they could measure, and possible explanations. The teacher invents the concept of osmosis, linking it to their language from Phase One, filling in any gaps in understanding, and using the correct scientific terminology. Next students are asked to design an experiment to deter-

TABLE 7–8   **Life Science Learning Cycle: Osmosis**

Process Skills: (List)

Standards Addressed: (check) SK ✔   SM ✔   CA___   SI___   PN___

Activity		Time
Activity 1	Phase One—Exploration Students observe dialysis tubing cells at learning stations. List observations, measurements, possible explanations.	15 minutes
Activity 2	Phase Two—Concept Invention Students share observations, ideas for measurement, possible explanations.	15 minutes
Activity 3	Phase Two—Concept Invention Teacher uses student responses, links student language to scientific language (diffusion, osmosis, osmotic pressure, hypertonic, hypotonic, isotonic).	15 minutes
Activity 4	Phase Three—Discovery/Application Students design experiment to determine the effect of three unknown solutions on a selected sample of live protozoa.	15 minutes
Activity 5	Phase Three—Discovery/Application Following teacher lab design approval, students conduct inquiry with unknown solutions.	30 minutes

mine the effects of three "unknown" solutions on a selected species of protozoan. Once designs are approved for a lab team, they proceed to the lab bench and conduct the inquiry as Phase Three of the learning cycle.

The unknown solutions vary in NaCl concentration. Each team may be assigned three different concentrations, or three identical concentrations, or some combination of isotonic, hypertonic, and/or hypotonic solutions. A nice twist here is to use *Paramecium caudatum* and let the contractile vacuole throw them for a loop!

COOPERATIVE STRATEGIES IN THE SCIENCE CLASSROOM

The Laboratory Experience

Science teachers who routinely incorporate laboratory experiences into the science curriculum are aware of the management considerations that affect the quality of learning that the laboratory affords science students. Layout of the lab, equipment available, class size, budget for expendable materials, prior exposure to technical and conceptual applications—all must be considered for optimal management of meaningful time at the "lab bench." As mentioned earlier in this chapter, the extended block can reduce problems created by class size, availability of materials and equipment, safety, and down time for setup and cleanup of the laboratory. The use of structured or formal cooperative learning planning for laboratory team approaches can increase opportunities for student learning and allow for positive interdependence and individual accountability.

In a traditional laboratory setting where students work in lab teams without formal cooperative structure, we may find one member of the team completing the laboratory tasks while other members go along for the ride as "academic parasites." We receive a completed lab report but have very little evidence that every member of the group has met the knowledge and method objectives established for the lab experience. We have only an informal or anecdotal record of the level of contribution made by each member of the lab team toward the completion of the project.

By incorporating cooperative learning structure into the lab team setting, we can ensure that students divide the labor equitably, assume individual and collective responsibility for the final laboratory report, resolve problems encountered that are inherent to work as scientists in a research team, and assess individual student performance in a tangible way.

When structuring a laboratory experience in which students will work as a member of a lab team, use the procedural guidelines delineated in Table 7–9.

We have seen the division of labor, collaborative learning, individual accountability assessments, and team performance assessments increase the active engagement of students in the science laboratory by making it more difficult for students to "hide" and let others do the work in the laboratory. This approach also increases on-task behavior and allows students to resolve team conflicts, leading them to more productive behavior in future lab experiences. As opposed to the traditional, unstructured "group work" approach that can permit "academic parasitism," the structured application of fundamental cooperative learning principles will promote "academic symbiosis." The extended block allows for a more structured approach to real cooperative learning in the laboratory setting.

TABLE 7–9   Cooperative Learning Structure for Laboratory Teams

1. *Roles and responsibilities:*
   Provide each team a division-of-labor listing. Have them decide who is responsible for each task. Once they have come to an agreement, each student places his or her signature next to the assigned role. For subsequent labs, roles rotate to another team member.

2. *Explanation of laboratory procedure and findings:*
   Once the laboratory investigation is completed, teams meet to explain the procedural steps followed, review the findings, and work to teach and/or review major outcomes of the lab.

3. *Completion of the written report:*
   All team members must have a completed copy of the final laboratory report. The teacher may randomly collect one copy to be graded. Students understand that every copy must be completed to the satisfaction of all members of the team.

4. *Individual lab quiz/performance evaluation:*
   In order to formally assess the progress of each student, students should individually complete a quiz and/or performance assessment related to the laboratory experience. A short quiz can be administered as an "open lab report" evaluation to determine how well each team member has mastered the concepts and process skills from the lab experience. When applicable, the laboratory can be followed by an assessment using hands-on lab performance stations. At these stations, students demonstrate individual performance using techniques and equipment incorporated in the lab they just finished.

5. *Student evaluation of individual and/or group performance:*
   Periodically, students may be asked to evaluate their own performance as a lab team member or to evaluate the performance of their peers. If problems have occurred, the team may be given the opportunity to suggest ways to resolve the problem and increase productivity.

The Unit Review

In addition to the effective use of cooperative strategies in the laboratory, cooperative learning can be used very effectively within the 90-minute block for a unit review session prior to a unit examination. The model illustrated in Table 7–10 incorporates a Roundrobin and variation of Numbered Heads within a 90-minute block. Students must come to class with a completed study guide for the unit of study on the day of the review. To increase the likelihood that students will have the study guide ready for review day, we encourage teachers to distribute the study guide on the first day of the unit, assigning small sections as homework each day. A quick check for completion of the guide over the course of the unit can help to ensure the successful application of the unit review method.

Depending on the length of the study guide and the nature of the questions, this review strategy can be compressed into a shorter time frame. However, the structure promotes individual accountability, team building, and evaluation of the social skill development of each team and the individual members. Note that this review format is limited to questions that require a short response. It may be more appropriate for some units of study than others. We find this far superior to whole-class question-and-answer reviews or "Jeopardy"-style reviews in which very few students actually have to be accountable or active. Another advantage of this form

TABLE 7–10 Roundrobin/Numbered Heads Unit Review Plan

Activity		*Time*
Activity 1	Explanation of Rules and Procedures The teacher provides an overview of the activity, establishes the social skills to be monitored for each team, and conveys how social skill points may be earned. Once clarified, teams are identified. Team composition is determined in advance by the teacher.	10 minutes
Activity 2	Roundrobin Students number off, and, beginning with student #1, read answers to the study guide question #1. Students discuss answers, and when consensus is reached, move to student #2 and question #2. The procedure is repeated until all questions have been reviewed. The teacher monitors each team for social skills and notes any questions that may need clarification.	25 minutes
Activity 3	Clarification The teacher directs a discussion on study guide questions noted during Activity 2.	10 minutes
Activity 4	Numbered Heads Once the students have had questions clarified, the teacher emphasizes that he or she will call one member of each team, by number, to the front of the class. The team representative will answer a question, randomly selected from the study guide and displayed visually. Each team member will write down a response to the question. Once this process is completed, the teacher reveals the correct answer, and awards one point for a correct answer. The points are accumulated by the team. The procedure is repeated by calling the "number twos" forward, and so on, until all review questions have been asked and answered.	30 minutes
Activity 5	Closure The teacher tallies team points and reveals the social skill acquisition for each team. Teams are directed to complete a self and/or peer evaluation of the team members. Final points of clarification may be made regarding the exam.	15 minutes

of review is that every member of the team must represent the team during the Numbered Heads. This variation of Numbered Heads Together will hold students accountable. They cannot depend on one team member to constantly carry the team.

Extension of the traditional 45-minute class period to an intensive block of 90 minutes allows us to optimize effective instructional strategies in the science classroom beyond traditional verification laboratory experiences. We are able to move our students through meaningful student-active science experiences and bring them to a closure.

TABLE 7–11 Putting Your Thoughts in Order: Science

1. List the most important concepts/skills that you want your students to understand/master before they walk out of your room at the end of the course.
2. List content/chapters to address each goal.
3. List effective activities now used to address each goal.
4. Indicate which concepts/skills you wish to address in more depth.
5. Think of ways in which you can personalize or contextualize each goal.
6. Consider various strategies that you might add to address each goal: cooperative learning, inquiry learning, study skill strategies. List them for each goal.

Goals	1. Concept Skills	2. Content Chapters	3. Current Activities	4. More Depth	5. Personalize, Contextualize	6. New Ideas
1.						
2.						
3.						
4.						
5.						
6.						
7.						
8.						
9.						
10.						

■ 8

Teaching Social Studies

THE EXTENDED-BLOCK schedule could be a dream come true for social studies teachers. For the first time in our lives, with the uninterrupted 90-minute period, we will finally have enough time to utilize the many resources and activities that are available to us. For the first time in our lives, we can show a 60-minute video during a single class period without having to stop it in the middle, or we can complete an inquiry lesson without having to stop the process midstream.

On the other hand, it is not surprising that a social studies teacher might be a little skeptical when considering the change to this type of teaching schedule. We may feel that we have a schedule that works for us, so why look for problems? However, when the teacher is given some guidance or direction on how to use this additional time per class period most effectively, it soon becomes obvious that this schedule is one that has many advantages for the social studies teacher.

ADVANTAGES OF THE BLOCK SCHEDULE

The strength of this schedule is that it does provide us with enough time to allow our students to participate seriously in the process of making informed decisions. When considering the many critical issues in the social sciences that require researching in the library via one of the electronic resources or that require in-depth study or discussion in the classroom, our students will now be able to search, research, and discuss these issues within one class meeting without being constrained by the typical 45-minute period.

Similarly, as we consider the advantages of the extended-block schedule for the social studies teacher, we need to look at the impact on class size. Under the traditional schedule, we are dealing with up to six or seven classes a day, with 25+ students per section. Under an extended block, we will be working with a maximum of three to four classes a day with 25+ students in each.

This change in schedule allows us finally to teach in ways that we know are most effective. When we consider the activities that could be a part of every lesson and the number of students with whom we will be dealing each day, the little extra initial effort to change our teaching techniques will be well worthwhile as an investment in making the most of this scheduling change. The variety of activities we will be able to utilize with our students will make the classroom environment more challenging and more relevant to our students' needs.

Research by Queen, Algozzine, and Eaddy (1996) documents a procedure used in Lincoln County, North Carolina, supporting a planning process for implementation of block scheduling previously detailed in Chapter 2 of this book. Similarities appear in implementation, especially in the material that dealt with the need for input from the community as well as the need for a concerted approach to facilitating the training of teachers to make best use of the extended teaching block. One of the points that the authors felt was especially necessary in achieving

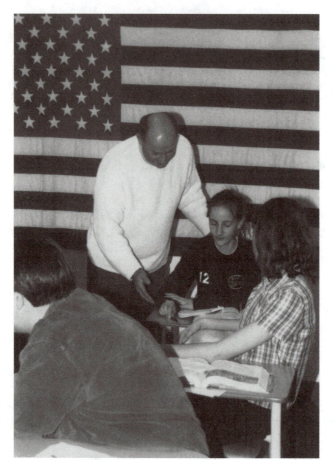

The time available in the extended-block schedule allows us to provide students with a quality learning experience.

acceptance of the scheduling alteration was the ongoing process of nonthreatening planned teacher observation to aid teachers in the process of changing teaching techniques. They saw that as the Lincoln County social studies teachers took ownership of the process, they began to feel increasingly comfortable in administering a more student-centered classroom.

The major strength of the Lincoln County approach is the reality of time: the longer class time allows greater flexibility in instructional activities. A ninth-grade American history teacher related an incident about locating a 42-minute film that really emphasized her point about Reconstruction issues in the post–Civil War South. Her frustration grew out of a time as well as a planning dilemma. With a 45-minute class period, she knew she could introduce the film and show a portion of it on the first day, then show the remainder of the film on the second day and start her planned follow-up discussion. She also knew that if she followed that schedule, she probably would be faced with some student absenteeism as well as some retention fallout from the students who had been present for only part of the two-day sequence. She then began to question herself: Was showing the film really worth the effort? She knew that the retention and the discussion would be much more fruitful if the whole activity could occur during one longer class period.

Similarly, for a unit on the court system, a valuable teaching activity would be a field trip to the local courthouse, 10 miles from the school. In an extended period of 90 minutes, students can travel to the site and, with a little cooperative planning with the next period teacher, have an on-site experience rather than missing the opportunity because of time.

When the teacher plans a cooperative learning lesson using the Jigsaw teaching technique with its four expert groups, time can be a problem. It is obvious that the expert groups need some time to prepare before they return to their home group. The "experts" need 20 to 30 minutes to research their question and then come to a consensus that they will be able to share in their home group. A typical 45-minute class period might allow time for one of the experts from each group to report back. By the time the class meets again, the original group structure might be changed because of student absenteeism. In addition, a minimum of 24 hours or a weekend will have passed, necessitating some review from the previous class session before the rest of the "experts" can report to their home groups. This teaching technique can certainly be much more successful if the whole process is implemented in one extended class period.

Productive library use is another result of the extended class schedule. In planning to take students to the library to utilize the library's various resources, including on-line searching of the available electronic databases, we contact the librarian to reserve a section of the library for whole-class use. The librarian reserves the available computer terminals for our students. She gives the class a quick refresher course highlighting new acquisitions and on-line protocol before students start using the materials. Only five students may complete their on-line search during the remainder of the typical 45-minute class period. Other classmates will have located some materials and begun to take some notes. Some will surely feel frustration. Perhaps members of the class can come back later in the day to work. Yet what about the student who can't return because of after-school activities? Even the student who has the time to return later in the day will be wasting valuable study time with a stop-again, start-again approach when following the traditional time schedule. The 45 additional minutes provided in the extended block can make all the difference!

Another advantage of the block schedule is the ability to do collaborative work with other faculty in our own subject area as well as outside of the social studies program. Many schools that use the extended-block schedule plan common preparation time for teachers within the same discipline. How beneficial it would be to have some real time to confer with our fellow teachers when requesting new materials, considering curriculum revision, or changing sequencing of courses!

In a district interested in cross-curricular planning, a block of 90 minutes to work with another faculty member can allow the social studies teacher to develop some creative approaches to link multiple curriculum areas. With a group of sophomores, the social studies teacher could teach World War II while the English teacher includes a section on modern world literature. Linking the reading of a novel such as *The Diary of Anne Frank* or Elie Wiesel's autobiography, *Night,* with the social studies teacher's consideration of the war would give students insight into the thoughts of a young adolescent living during that time period. A writing assignment could be a part of the evaluation of this unit, with the social studies teacher reading the paper for historical accuracy and the English teacher evaluating the essay for grammar and composition.

Another advantage that the block schedule provides for a social studies teacher is the opportunity to do more frequent formative student testing. If students are made more accountable for their learning, they often feel more ownership of the end results. For example, in teaching a World Civilizations course, we introduce students to Italian Renaissance art. After giving the class an introduction to the characteristics of the Italian art of the period, we can provide them with examples of noted works of art and have them identify and describe in their own words how the characteristics are represented in each work. Doing an activity like this one clears up any misconceptions in their understanding before they leave the class for the day.

Another related advantage is that this schedule gives teachers more control over their own teaching. With the 90-minute class period, teachers can include lessons that give the students a greater chance to experience an in-depth study of the topic of the day. For example, after we have introduced the decade of the 1930s, we can give students the opportunity to understand the impact of FDR's fireside chats by playing an audiotape of one of the chats so that the class experiences the impact of this approach to influencing public opinion. In contrast with a 45-minute block of time, by the time we introduce the concept and play the tape, the class time is over. With the extended block, we can provide the rationale, play the chat, and still have class time for students to analyze how public opinion was influenced by the media available at the time.

In addition to planning lessons that expand the theme of the Great Depression, the New Deal, and other events of the 1930s, we will not only give students background knowledge of the events leading up to this period, but we also can include a variety of other meaningful activities. Students can use the material that they have gained through their assigned readings or other media presentations to develop mini-dramas interpreting workers organizing a union or presenting a day in the life of a young person working in a Civilian Conservation Corps camp. Our students can then complete a writing assignment in which they give their own interpretations of the impact of the New Deal programs.

As mentioned earlier, this scheduling approach requires some rethinking of traditional approaches to planning. With the extended block as a part of our routine, we will become teachers who can really delve into a topic and give our students a quality learning experience. The first step is to outline the major topics that must be covered for every subject assigned during a typical academic year. Then formulate some of the key activities to include in the lessons. Third, think of each lesson as a series of at least three activities. Then consider how long each of these activities will take to implement properly. Those who have been successful in teaching on the block often state that thinking in segments of lessons, rather than in whole lessons, makes the planning less overwhelming.

In beginning the actual planning, we might first review the most current curriculum standards that shape social studies teaching. The most recent standards released by the National Council for the Social Studies, entitled *Expectations of Excellence: Curriculum Standards for Social Studies* (1994), defines social studies as the integrated study of the social sciences and humanities to promote civic competence. Within the school program, social studies provides coordinated, systematic study drawing on such disciplines as anthropology, archaeology, economics, geography, history, law, philosophy, political science, psychology, religion, and sociology, as well as appropriate content from the humanities, mathematics, and natural sciences (*Standards*, 1994, p. 3).

In the introduction to the standards, the primary purpose of social studies is further defined as helping young people develop the ability to make informed and reasoned decisions for the public good as citizens of a culturally diverse, democratic society in an interdependent world (*Standards*, 1994, p. 3).

Supporting this premise, the standards further encapsulate the essence of social studies into the ten strands or themes shown in Table 8–1.

As is further explained in the introduction to the standards, the curriculum strands are interrelated for a reason.

TABLE 8–1 Ten Thematic Strands in Social Studies

Social Studies programs should include experiences that provide for . . .

I.	Culture	The study of culture and cultural diversity
II.	Time, Continuity, and Change	The study of the ways human beings view themselves in and over time
III.	People, Places, and Environments	The study of people, places, and environments
IV.	Individual Development and Identity	The study of individual development and identity
V.	Individuals, Groups, and Institutions	The study of interactions among individuals, groups, and institutions
VI.	Power, Authority and Governance	The study of how people create and change structures of power, authority, and governance
VII.	Production, Distribution, and Consumption	The study of how people organize for the production, distribution, and consumption of goods and services
VIII.	Science, Technology, and Society	The study of relationships among science, technology, and society
IX.	Global Connections	The study of global connections and interdependence
X.	Civic Ideals and Practices	The study of ideals, principles, and practices of citizenship in a democratic republic

Source: National Council of the Social Studies, *Expectations of Excellence* (pp. 19–30). Used with permission.

To understand culture, for example, students need to understand time, continuity, and changes; the relationship among people, places, and environments; and civic ideals and practices. Second, the thematic strands draw from all the social science disciplines and other related disciplines and fields of scholarly study to build a framework for state and local curriculum design (*Standards*, 1994, p. 15).

As discussed in the standards, appropriate sequencing is defined, and significant concepts to be taught are outlined as performance expectations.

With the guidance that has been provided by the National Council for the Social Studies, today's social studies teacher is challenged to meet the goals that have been set.

PLANNING FOR INSTRUCTION

Let us now consider the actual planning for instruction in the extended block. We will need to attack this planning just as we would any other challenge. We must realize that we have the necessary knowledge base to draw on because of our previous teaching experience. We also have the curriculum guidelines established in our own district, as well as the goals that have been provided by the National Council for the Social Studies. Taking the data that we have gathered, we can make a general list of all the topics and correlating activities necessary to meet those goals and guidelines for the academic semester or year in the extended block. The third step is to approximate the actual time it will take to teach the selected topics.

We need to be sure to include activities that will make our classrooms interactive ones, yet ones that also will allow our students to take ownership of their own learning. We must make a point of including activities that will challenge our students and cause them to use their previously developed critical thinking skills. Refreshing our memories about the challenge previously given to us by the National Council for the Social Studies, we must choose activities that will challenge our students, yet give meaning and better understanding of the subject explored. Fourth, we need to take some time to consider how we will plan to evaluate student learning. Remember, we have just plotted out the sequence for the block, so the next logical task would be to plan what methods to use to evaluate these topics. We must be sure to review these previously developed data so that we can be sure that we will be providing for a variety of methods to evaluate student progress.

After doing the necessary long-range planning, it is time to plan for the individual lesson. The key to successful teaching in the extended block is to think of every lesson that we plan as utilizing the concept of thinking in a series of threes. We first must include an introductory or set induction activity, then an actual teaching activity, and finally an evaluating or transitional activity before starting the sequence again. The transition between activities can easily provide the necessary flow material to make each lesson work to its best advantage.

First look at the type of introductory activity that we can use. Why not place a review question or a question to ponder on the board before the students enter your classroom? This activity, often referred to as a "bellringer" or "hook," can set a positive instructional tone for an entire class period. What this activity actually does is focus students on the topic at hand and give the teacher the time to handle some of the clerical activities that need to be done when a new class of students arrives. After giving the students three to five minutes to come up with a response, the teacher can continue the class by asking the question orally to the group as a focus or starting point for the period.

It is now time to investigate the content of the day. We can give a short overview on the new topic for the day, providing the necessary background information to help students deal with the day's topic. If the focus is to be on the types of propaganda that a student might face daily, the teacher can project several examples of propaganda on a screen to introduce the variety that can be present in the media. The third activity, used to evaluate, can be a small-group activity in which the teacher can provide the class with examples for small groups to analyze to determine whether the groups are able to identify types of propaganda.

Next, the teacher can have a large-group discussion where the class can review what has been analyzed as a transition to the second part of the class period. At this time, the teacher can have the students again divide into small groups to develop a poster or a short skit utilizing propaganda. With this activity, the students will be able to show their understanding of the topic and the teacher can formatively evaluate their progress toward meeting the daily lesson objective. To do all of what has been accomplished in one class period would probably take several class periods under the traditional schedule. The teacher would only be able to complete the first three activities in a normal 45-minute class period. In that case the teacher probably would have to backtrack and review during the first portion of the next class period, before she could assign the application activity.

Other "teaching" activities we can include in the middle section of the first sequence of the lesson can be a teacher-initiated demonstration, a cooperative learning activity, media reinforcement, a simulation or game, or a classroom discussion.

Other "evaluative" activities might include a quick formative oral review, a short writing assignment, a previously assigned oral report, or a case study.

TABLE 8–2   General Lesson Plan Format for Social Studies

Goal/objective for the period:	
Introductory activity:	Time: _____
Activity I	Time: _____
Evaluative Activity or Activity 2	Time: _____
Activity 3 or transition	Time: _____
Activity 4	Time: _____
Activity 5	Time: _____
Resources or materials needed:	

Above all, when teachers are planning for the extended block, we must be prepared to include a variety of activities in each plan and be sure to change activities frequently throughout the period. As is common knowledge, the attention span of a typical secondary student is such that activities must be varied and changed frequently for students to meet their full learning potential.

The general lesson plan format with minimal alteration previously introduced in Chapter 6 should work very effectively for a social studies teacher teaching in the extended block. The format is reintroduced via Table 8–2 for reference.

In this section be sure to include any handouts, overhead transparencies, supplemental readings, videos, or rubrics that will be necessary to teach an effective lesson.

FIGURE 8–1   Planning in Chunks of Time: Building an Integrated Social Studies Plan

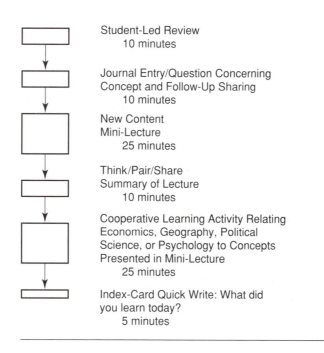

Student-Led Review
10 minutes

Journal Entry/Question Concerning
Concept and Follow-Up Sharing
10 minutes

New Content
Mini-Lecture
25 minutes

Think/Pair/Share
Summary of Lecture
10 minutes

Cooperative Learning Activity Relating
Economics, Geography, Political
Science, or Psychology to Concepts
Presented in Mini-Lecture
25 minutes

Index-Card Quick Write: What did
you learn today?
5 minutes

After the teacher has determined the objectives/goals and the time frame that is needed to accomplish the objectives, it is time to develop the final plan. For additional guidance in planning, see Figure 8–1 and Table 8–6 at the end of this chapter.

GUIDELINES FOR EFFECTIVE IMPLEMENTATION

Traditionally, resources such as filmstrips, photographs, videos, transparencies, and slides have been valuable supplemental devices in the typical social studies classroom. When we choose to use these resources, we realize we are providing another means of clarification for our students. The option to include any of the wide range of tools currently available to us allows us to provide additional aural as well as visual reinforcement for concepts that might be hard for the typical student to comprehend. Even with the almost universal availability of television and video cassette recorders in a typical home, many of these resources are missed by our students unless we specifically point out their relevance. What we must remember is that we, as the teachers, do possess the expertise to utilize these media to their best purposes.

Consider the lengthy video cited earlier in this chapter. A video of similar length could have introduced our students to aspects of the Mexican culture. Considering that this culture may be very different from our own, by playing this video without sound for a portion of the extended block, we could ask our students for their first impressions, with a simple question: "What did you see?" After brainstorming some ideas, the video could be rerun and the students would be instructed to focus on concepts that had been introduced by other class members. In an extended block, this activity could be accomplished within one class period.

Another media experience that might be better accomplished in the extended block would be an in-depth discussion of slave sale placards replicated from nineteenth-century newspapers available in many large public libraries. Depending on the number of examples that are available for analysis, students could be divided into groups. Each group could then be given an example plus a set of questions to consider while doing their analysis. After each group reaches a consensus, they would be able to present their findings within the confines of one class period (Table 8–3).

An analysis of selected political cartoons could also follow a format similar to the one outlined here. The cartoons found in newspapers and magazines may dramatize a political issue more effectively than any narrative could ever do. When introducing this medium, a set of questions such as the following should be presented to the students to aid them in their analysis.

1. What do you see portrayed in the cartoon?
2. What does each character in the cartoon symbolize?
3. Analyze the cartoonist's choice of background.
4. Devise an alternative caption for the cartoon.

A teaching technique that many social studies teachers feel can be more effectively used after a school district adopts the block schedule is the cooperative learning teaching method. This teaching method allows the social studies teacher the luxury of dividing classes into small heterogeneous learning groups where the students will have the opportunity to investigate a specific aspect of the subject under consideration in a less formal learning environment.

TABLE 8–3 A Plan Using Media as the Basis for Instruction

Activity		Time
Activity 1	Introductory Activity The students silently read a newspaper article that documents a slave auction reenactment. They write their thoughts in their notebooks.	15 minutes
Activity 2	Mini-lecture/discussion The teacher provides background information by displaying two examples of slave advertisements reproduced from southern newspapers.	10 minutes
Activity 3	Cooperative Learning Students are divided into groups of four to review other slave advertisements. Students will analyze teacher-prepared questions and develop conclusions.	15 minutes
Activity 4	Guided Discussion Each cooperative learning group will present its conclusion. Whole-group sharing of their observations follows. The teacher lists pertinent findings on the board.	25 minutes
Activity 5	Application and Expansion Students will take the information introduced and develop a short essay documenting any understandings gained.	Remainder of the period

A good example of effective use of cooperative learning would be a type of three-step interview. Suppose we are studying the Boston Massacre. Our aim is for our students to realize some of the ethical issues the colonists faced during this period of American history. We have focused our students by describing the events prior to the massacre as well as a description of the actual massacre. We then could divide our class into groups of four; then regroup the groups of four into two pairs. Within each pair, have one student act as an interviewer and the other as the interviewee. For three to four minutes, the interviewer will ask a series of questions focusing on who is in the right in the Boston Massacre, the American citizens or the British troops?

After the initial interview, the interviewee changes places with the interviewer, and the same questions are posed. The two pairs regroup into their initial group of four. Next would come a period of group sharing with a large-group discussion. The teacher would then provide further detail of the events that occurred in the aftermath of the massacre.

The final activity of the class period would include a short in-class writing assignment and a period of active student review. The conclusion would be that both sides were probably at fault; however, through the cooperative discussion, the students would be able to begin to understand the gray areas in this controversy (Table 8–4).

Another cooperative learning activity using the theme of the American Revolution might be a Think, Pair, Share activity where the students could debate the rightness or wrongness of the people's right to participate in revolution. When students think about such issues as, "Is it ever right for people to revolt against their government?" and "Under what conditions would it be right?" and then share as

TABLE 8–4   A Plan Using Cooperative Learning

Activity		Time
Activity 1	Mini-lecture by the teacher highlighting the events leading up to March 5, 1770, the Boston Massacre.	10 minutes
Activity 2	Cooperative Learning Activity using three-step interview.	15 minutes
Activity 3	Large-group discussion sharing hypotheses.	25 minutes
Activity 4	Mini-lecture: Teacher reviews aftermath of the Boston Massacre, including the trial and the organization of the Committees of Correspondence.	15 minutes
Activity 5	Students write a one-minute paper highlighting who is to blame.	10 minutes
Activity 6	Active student review conducted by the teacher.	Remainder of the period

a pair and as a group, they will become better able to understand the rationale for radical action. A good relevancy check could come when we make a connection to actions in the world today.

Simulations can be accomplished more effectively when we have additional teaching time available to us. Simulation can be used to examine social issues and can be a method to provide another perspective on an issue facing individuals or groups during the historical period that is currently being examined in class. For example, when we are considering the impact of the Great Depression, simulations can be used to help our students understand the Depression's impact on the American people. Singer, Dircks, and Turner (1996) describe samples of dramatic settings that can be used, including a discussion of the lives of members of a family living in a Hooverville, or a day in the life of a youth working in a Civilian Conservation Corps camp.

As we set up a simulation, we need to guide our students to a successful final product. Martorella (1991) describes a five-step process toward successful implementation of a simulation. He reviews our responsibility first to choose issues that our students can envision; then to guide our students to develop a simple reenactment of the event through the process of assigning roles, doing the actual enactment, and engaging in analysis or debriefing. We must realize that a successful simulation will occur only when we guide our students to analyze and then verbalize their feelings after participating in such an experience (Table 8–5).

We spend a great deal of time teaching our students the facts about a particular incident in history. As another approach, why not take our students to a location similar in terrain to the site of the battle and have them reenact the conflict? For example, students might conduct a planned reenactment of a Civil War battle. Prepare each of the armies with the basic background information; then let them fight the battle as they envision it actually occurred. After the "battle," have the students debrief by writing what went through their minds as they faced the challenge of battle.

A case study also can be used very effectively by the social studies teacher in the extended block. We are all aware of the printed case study, where we read an account of a single issue in history from a variety of points of view. Consider examining different newspaper accounts of the same incident, such as the Japanese attack on Pearl Harbor. Have students compare the number of casualties reported,

TABLE 8–5 A Plan Using Simulation

Activity		Time
Activity 1	Teacher introduces concept of simulation and possible topics to be simulated.	10 minutes
Activity 2	Student groups are developed and students are given time to brainstorm and do research with materials readily available in the classroom.	40 minutes
Activity 3	Students present short simulations in class.	20 minutes
Activity 4	Teacher leads discussion in which students analyze the impact of the Great Depression on the American people.	Remainder of Period

the failed negotiations prior to the attack, or the reported reactions by the political leaders of the period. The focusing of the activity, the reading of the accounts, the small-group analysis, and the large-group discussion all can be accomplished during a 90-minute class period.

As social studies teachers, we have to take advantage of the opportunities this extended block can give to our teaching. It is true that we will have to reexamine our teaching methods and the sequencing of our classes, and we may have to adopt some teaching approaches that may seem a little foreign at first; however, when we consider how we are now better meeting our students' learning needs, the final result—a more student-active environment—will be well worth the effort!

TABLE 8–6 Putting Your Thoughts in Order: Social Studies

1. List the most important concepts/skills that you want your students to understand/master before they walk out of your room at the end of the course.
2. List content/chapters to address each goal.
3. List effective activities now used to address each goal.
4. Indicate which concepts/skills you wish to address in more depth.
5. Think of ways in which you can personalize or contextualize each goal.
6. Consider various strategies that you might add to address each goal: cooperative learning, inquiry learning, study skill strategies. List them for each goal.

Goals	1. Concept Skills	2. Content Selections	3. Current Activities	4. More Depth	5. Personalize, Contextualize	6. New Ideas
1.						
2.						
3.						
4.						
5.						
6.						
7.						
8.						
9.						
10.						

■ 9
Teaching Mathematics

AS POINTED OUT in Chapter 2, administrators and teachers alike need to remember that a successful transition from the traditional 45- or 50-minute class period to the extended block requires careful inservicing as well as team planning. For example, David Petersen of the Lander, Wyoming, schools emphasizes that his district took two years to train teachers and gather community support before implementing the block (*NCTM News Bulletin*, September 1996). Craig Auten (1995) of Walled Lake Central High in Oakland County, Michigan, points out the following:

> *We used a committee to restructure our day. One important feature of our plan is a Wednesday A.M. teacher meeting that lasts two hours. It was from here that retraining our staff occurred. The important thing we found out was not the time but how you deliver the information.*

Of all the teachers moving into block scheduling, math teachers may encounter the most difficulty because of the traditional nature of mathematics instruction that we have experienced in our own training and which to a great extent we carry over into our own teaching. We may be uncomfortable with a student-active classroom, preferring to follow a more traditional sequence of teacher-directed homework review, lecture, demonstration of new material, and assignment of samples for students to complete. We also worry that we cannot force students to accelerate their learning of algebraic concepts, that they need two semesters of exposure in order to assimilate the crucial aspects of algebra. It concerns us that we may have less time to review previous course content within this new schedule. Also, in the seven-period traditional schedule, we have not had time to explore new computer applications and programs useful for teaching concepts in more depth. So, for us, preliminary inservicing and the time to sit down with other math teachers to discuss strategies useful in the changing of our approaches to teaching algebra, geometry, trigonometry, and calculus are crucial.

ADVANTAGES IN THE MATH CLASSROOM

The block provides distinct advantages for the math classroom. For example, teachers can go into more depth in the extended time period. Teachers can nurture problem solving by providing activities that require critical thinking and that engage students in student-active investigations through which they develop deeper comprehension. We can plan and implement inquiry-based lessons that give the students opportunities to construct meaning based on prior knowledge and experiences.

In addition, the extended block can provide the time to include reality-based applications. Mulligan (1997) notes:

I have students do a real-world project with area businesses that requires mathematical abilities and computer support that many small businesses don't have access to.
Some of the projects include the following:

1. *Which kind of heater (gas or electric) should the "Y" buy for the pool? Both were linear functions, but one had a larger y-intercept and lesser slope. Students analyzed at what year a larger initial investment would pay off.*
2. *A survey regarding optimum usage of a piece of property. The analysis of the results supplemented the unit on statistics.*
3. *An analysis of ski resort usage to determine if the resort should expand facilities, work force, or buy more skis.*

All of these topics supplemented topics taught in the Algebra II curriculum and really increased interest in the study of math. They would have been difficult to do in a 45-minute period.

A third advantage of the extended block in the math classroom is the potential for cross-curricular planning. Teachers can structure labs to apply math concepts directly to experimental situations. The concept of exponential growth, for example, can be explored in a lab experiment in which the students measure and record the growth of "germs" in Petri dishes over a week's time. Students can then be challenged to apply that laboratory information to related problems, such as the effect of altering the time allotment on exponential growth. Interdisciplinary planning can allow students to apply math concepts to many other curriculum areas as well.

Another distinct advantage for math teachers and students is the use of technology. In the 45- or 50-minute class, introducing the day's tasks, moving students to the computer lab, and completing a meaningful computer application can be difficult at best. The extended block provides the time to integrate computer lab assignments into the day's activities. It encourages the use of graphing calculators and the use of manipulatives.

Commenting from his position as math teacher in the Urban School of San Francisco, Henri Picciotto (1995) comments, "It's entirely a question of how you use the longer period, which gives you the opportunity to bore the kids for longer with lectures and drills, or the opportunity to get them engaged with lessons involving cooperative learning and labs."

MATHEMATICS STANDARDS

Mathematics teachers beginning to plan for the extended block should consider the philosophy and the standards created by the National Council of Teachers of Mathematics in 1989. The curriculum outlined by the NCTM (Table 9–1) emphasizes the teaching of topics in a much more in-depth manner than occurs in the traditional curriculum. Although the traditional curriculum divisions of algebra, geometry, trigonometry, and functions remain as the most important facets of the curriculum, the NCTM encourages the use of a variety of teaching strategies and technologies. Students are expected to be able to clarify processes, translate symbols, and apply concepts learned. The standards emphasize the need for students to increase their skills in investigation and in the construction of new ideas, and to learn to predict and to utilize concepts learned in the solving of new problems. This approach to the teaching of math also differs from the traditional approach in

TABLE 9–1   NCTM Curriculum Standards

1. Mathematics as Problem Solving
2. Mathematics as Communication
3. Mathematics as Reasoning
4. Mathematical Connections
5. Algebra
6. Functions
7. Geometry from a Synthetic Perspective
8. Geometry from an Algebraic Perspective
9. Trigonometry
10. Statistics
11. Probability
12. Discrete Mathematics
13. Conceptual Underpinnings of Calculus
14. Mathematical Structure

Source: National Council of Teachers of Mathematics Commission on Standards for School Mathematics, *Curriculum and Evaluation Standards for School Mathematics* (Reston, VA: Author, 1989), p. iv.

the emphasis on the use of real-life problems. All students are to have the opportunity to learn mathematical concepts and skills that will allow them to achieve success in their personal lives as well as in the world of work and in their roles as contributors to the well-being of our society.

Because the extended block promotes the use of a variety of teaching strategies and encourages student involvement in and ownership of the problem-solving processes, planning for this longer class period is a perfect time for giving renewed attention to the mathematics standards.

PLANNING FOR THE EXTENDED BLOCK

The standards indicate the need to combine lectures and whole-group strategies with smaller group activities. NCTM asks us to integrate technology such as graphing calculators and computer programs in addition to other hands-on strategies involving the use of manipulatives. They urge us to pose more divergent questions and to encourage higher expectations. In implementing the standards, we need to consider the use of writing in the classroom, a greater emphasis on small-group activities, the inclusion of authentic real-world problem solving to a greater extent than is usually explored in the traditional classroom, and a greater integration of technology as a mathematical tool. As noted in *Prisoners of Time* (1994), students must have more instruction in the process of studying effectively, the use of study skills strategies, and the knowledge of how to learn what they must learn.

As professionals and experts in mathematics, we know which concepts demand the most time for students to grasp. The first step, then, is to decide which concepts will be presented in more depth with practice time and related applications, and which can be covered in less depth. In addition, we have to analyze our sequence of courses for areas of redundancy. With adequate planning time, the mathematics department as a group can complete this initial step for each course offering. In this way, the professionals who know their district and their students best can make more informed decisions about the time emphasis for skills most needed by their students. Combining this information with application of the *Standards* for grades 9–12 will provide the basic road map for teachers to travel into this uncharted territory.

The general planning format presented in Chapter 6 can be used as a skeleton outline so that math teachers can begin to think about teaching in a sequence of three to five activities per class period. Initial feedback from some math teachers indicates that the block is wonderful for the advanced student, but it is difficult to keep students who show less interest in mathematics on task and involved for the longer class period (Baxter, 1997). The five-activity plan may be useful for less motivated students because we can include more real-world application and hands-on activities to capture interest and to provide in-depth experiences for these students. For general planning, see also Figure 9–1 and Table 9–13 at the end of this chapter.

In considering instruction in the extended-block period, math teachers can look to techniques appropriate to many curriculum areas and adaptable to the mathematics topics taught. Strategies such as cooperative learning, inquiry-based lessons, multiple study skills techniques, and writing applications are effective and efficient for the mathematics content of a secondary program. We must carefully plan transitions, as well, in order to keep the less motivated students focused during the block.

INQUIRY-BASED LEARNING STRATEGIES WITH MATH INSTRUCTION

The extended block gives us more time to develop higher order thinking skills in our students. Inquiry learning strategies, as described in Chapter 4, provide the structure to address this development.

Table 9–2 shows an Inquiry Training application to a geometry class in which the teacher has taught classification of geometric shapes. The goal of the inquiry is for students to learn a logical thought pathway that will allow them to identify an unknown geometric shape.

The process outlined in Table 9–2 is repeated for other geometric shapes. This inquiry will serve as an excellent review of the properties of various geometric figures.

The Inquiry Training model can also be applied as an introduction to new content and mathematical skill development. In teaching the concept of slope as conveyed by rise and run, the teacher poses the following problem to the class:

> *A carpenter is given the job of building a set of stairs for a new house. Your task is to ask me a series of yes/no questions in order to gain enough information that will allow you to diagram, to scale, the stairway.*

In this inquiry, the stairway is a standard straight run that connects the first story and second story of the home. Questions will have to determine this and relate to rise and run of a set of stairs.

Phases Two and Three follow the syntax of Inquiry Training. Once the students have determined the parameters of the problem and have arrived at a close approximation of the dimensions of the staircase, Phase Four begins. In this phase, the teacher explains the concept of slope as a function of rise and run, relating it to the stairs. Students then construct a scale drawing of the stairway.

Phase Five requires students to analyze the process of inquiry that they followed. They classify questions as general and specific, place them in a more logical order, and sort out irrelevant questions.

TABLE 9–2   Identification of Geometric Shapes: Inquiry Training

Phase One	The teacher explains the rules of inquiry (Chapter 4) and poses the problem: "Each of these cards has a drawing of a single geometric figure. You must ask me a series of questions in order to identify the figure." (The card selected is a parallelogram.)
Phase Two	Students begin to collect data by asking questions. For example, Q: Is it a circle? NO Q: Is it a polygon? YES Q: Does it have more than 6 sides? NO
Phase Three	Student questions begin to narrow based on the series of questions asked in Phase One. The questions begin to isolate the variables. For example, Q: Does it have 4 sides? YES Q: Does it have any equal sides? YES Q: Does it have two equal adjoining sides? NO The teacher asks for hypotheses when students appear to be ready. For example, H1: It is a rectangle. H2: It is a trapezoid. H3: It is a parallelogram. The students are asked to agree or disagree with each hypothesis and may decide that they need to ask more questions.
Phase Four	For this inquiry, the teacher confirms the correct identification, and reviews the data collected from the questions and answers from Phases Two and Three that support the hypothesis.
Phase Five	Students are told to label the questions as general or specific, and then to place them in a more logical order. This makes the logical path a conscious one.

As we plan for the extended block, we can also add variety and higher level thinking skills by employing the inquiry-based learning cycle. As described in Chapter 4, the learning cycle utilizes the three phases of exploration, invention, and, in this case, application. In an Integrated Mathematics I lesson on transformational geometry, the students employ critical thinking to form hypotheses about the movement of two figures (Table 9–3). The teacher employs the mini-lecture and independent practice to help students translate and rotate figures on a coordinate plane and to rotate a figure on polar graph paper.

COOPERATIVE LEARNING

In the traditional mathematics classroom, students work individually on problems given to them by the teacher, who circulates among the students offering assistance and redirection as needed. Each student attempts to apply newly learned concepts to arrive at a predetermined solution alone, often meeting with points of frustration and confusion on the way to success. The frustration and confusion clear only when the teacher arrives to set the student back on the right track. This

TABLE 9–3   Transformational Geometry and the Learning Cycle

Phase One	In a heads-together activity, students are asked to hypothesize about the movement of two figures on a coordinate plane based on their prior knowledge. They are to write down strategies used to develop their solution.	30 minutes
	The teacher and students discuss their hypotheses. At this time, the teacher also shows the students the thought process she used to solve the problem and introduces transformation.	
Phase Two	The teacher lectures on translation.	20 minutes
	A quick write asks students to review what they have learned with a partner, then to share their journal entries with the class.	5 minutes
	The teacher then presents a mini-lecture on rotations.	15 minutes
Phase Three	Using a Think, Pair, Share, the teacher gives students three problems to do individually. They will compare answers with their partners. They will then share their answers with the class, explaining their work. (Baxter, 1996)	20 minutes

necessitates waiting on the part of students and moving double time on the part of the teacher. Try as we might, in a traditional 45- or 50-minute class period, one teacher cannot always get to every student for consultation and redirection. Students may therefore leave class with a new concept that is only partly understood or completely misunderstood. Homework problems are then done incorrectly or not at all, as frustration takes over, and the next day the cycle begins again.

Cooperative learning strategies used in math instruction in the extended-block period can help the teacher to rewrite that scenario and break the cycle of confusion. They allow us to make effective use of class instruction time, our time spent directly with students, and students' time spent on practicing new concepts. By establishing cooperative groups as described in Chapter 3, the secondary math teacher can have a time-efficient, task-oriented approach to instruction.

Many cooperative learning strategies described in Chapter 3 are appropriate for the mathematics curriculum. As you recall, Roundrobin is a cooperative learning strategy that is appropriate for skills practice and review because it involves a small group of students in a collaborative procedure in which each contributes one part to the whole. This allows a multiple-step process to be dissected and rebuilt by the contributions and support of one's peers. Table 9–4 shows a Roundrobin activity requiring students to calculate simple interest.

TABLE 9–4   Calculating Interest

Distribute one worksheet to each group with the problem listed below. Have one student read the story aloud, then suggest the first step in the solution. The student to the reader's left writes the first step, then passes to his left so that student can make the initial calculation and suggest the next step. The process continues around the circle until the problem is solved.

Taylor Swanson opens a savings account that earns 6% interest annually. After one year he receives $48.00 in interest. How much money had Taylor deposited to open the account?

TABLE 9–5   Numbered Heads Together: Geometry

Place students in groups of three, giving each person in each group a number from 1 to 3. Read aloud the following problem:

> *You know that an isosceles triangle has at least two angles with the same measure. Each member of your group needs to be able to tell me what the measures of the base angles of an isosceles triangle are if the vertex angle measures 40 degrees.*

Allow groups to discuss for a preannounced amount of time. Then call one number (1, 2, or 3) and have those students stand. Select one of the standing students to give the response.

TABLE 9–6   Think-Pair-Share for Equations as Relations

Place students in separate seats, but close to a partner. Provide the entire class with the following problem:

$$\text{Solve } y = 2x + 3 \text{ if the domain is } (-5, -3, -1, 0, 1, 3, 4, 7, 9).$$

Allow students a set time to solve the problem. When time has expired, ask students to turn to their partner and take turns sharing their solutions. When all have shared, the teacher may ask volunteers to share their response with the rest of the class.

Numbered Heads Together is another cooperative learning strategy, which was discussed in Chapter 3, to encourage review and skills practice, both important activities in the math classroom. In small groups, students can safely discuss processes and solutions before risking an answer in front of the entire class. Table 9–5 gives an example of a Numbered Heads Together activity to review the processes needed for finding the measure of angles.

The Think-Pair-Share strategy is most appropriate in the math classroom because teachers need to have students practice the application of new mathematical processes under their watchful eyes. It is important to supervise their initial practice with new concepts so errors can be corrected and misunderstandings clarified before students go off to use the skills on their own. The three steps of the Think-Pair-Share technique allow students to practice the new skills with the support of peers and their teacher. Table 9–6 provides an example for applying information gained concerning equations as relations.

STUDY SKILLS

Although math is often viewed as the study of numbers, mathematics actually has a language that students must learn to read if they hope to learn. Symbols frequently replace words, numbers represent words, and abstract concepts are described by the use of symbols and numbers instead of words. As students progress through the levels of mathematics from arithmetic to algebra to calculus, this language often seems increasingly complex and confusing. However, the language of mathematics does not need to be a barrier to understanding. If students are able to read their mathematics materials just as they read other content material, they will be able to focus on the mathematical processes, the logic and critical thinking that are important to understanding and enjoying math.

The Directed Reading Activity (DRA) is a study skills technique especially suited to mathematics instruction because it guides the students in every step of the process. The DRA involves four steps, which can be used with most math textbooks. In the first step, the teacher provides a brief overview of the content to be studied and the application of the topic to the course or, better yet, to students' lives outside the classroom. During the second step, the vocabulary needed to understand the topic and processes is examined. This is not a cursory examination of the letter composition and pronunciation of the word, but an active involvement with the word, including its literal meaning, historical development, and relationship to the day's lesson. Third, the students read, usually silently, the text material in the books. Finally, the students participate in an activity requiring them to use the information from the book in a short application task. This task can be completed alone or with a partner. It can involve a worksheet or manipulatives used to demonstrate the concept just discussed. Many math teachers extend the DRA by providing an independent task for students to complete on their own as homework. This is an appropriate approach but should not replace Step 4 of the DRA, which allows students to apply immediately the information gained under the watchful eye of the teacher. Table 9–7 provides an example of a Directed Reading Activity for an algebra lesson.

Graphic organizers, explained in Chapter 5, are also effective in helping students understand mathematical processes. Mathematical procedures are very precise and consist of small steps connected in a specific pattern. Being able to identify the smaller components of a math process makes the entire process easier to understand. Graphic organizers allow students to analyze the steps of any math process by giving them a visual representation of the steps involved in the process. Table 9–8 provides an example of a graphic organizer for the mathematics curriculum.

TABLE 9–7   DRA for Solving Percent Problems

Step 1—Overview	The teacher explains to the students that they are going to learn how to solve percent problems. The teacher clarifies that *percent* refers to the amount out of 100 and is used to mean per hundred or hundredths. The teacher shows a card with 100 pennies taped to it and explains that these pennies represent 100% of a dollar.
Step 2—Vocabulary	The students are given word cards with the terms *percentage, base, rate,* and *proportion* on them. The teacher then writes on the board, $$\frac{75}{100}$$ The teacher tells a story about the number of relatives who actually attended the past family reunion. As the teacher tells the story, using the vocabulary on the students' word cards, the students are to place them in a line on their desks. The story concludes with the teacher asking student volunteers to place word cards next to their appropriate symbols on the board.
Step 3—Reading	The teacher then directs students to pages 85–88 of their text and tells them to read silently, looking for the vocabulary just discussed.
Step 4—Application	Students are put into pairs. Each pair is given a set of problem cards and a sheet of paper for calculations and final answers. Students work together to solve the percent problems on the cards as the teacher monitors.

TABLE 9–8   Graphic Organizer for Geometry

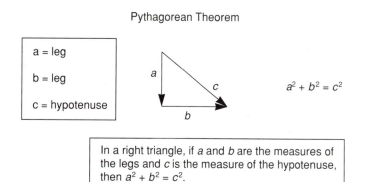

Pythagorean Theorem

| a = leg |
| b = leg |
| c = hypotenuse |

$a^2 + b^2 = c^2$

In a right triangle, if *a* and *b* are the measures of the legs and *c* is the measure of the hypotenuse, then $a^2 + b^2 = c^2$.

Explaining a math procedure in words helps students to understand the sequential steps clearly.

WRITING OPPORTUNITIES IN THE MATH CLASSROOM

Writing is an extremely complex task requiring total concentration. Because of the concentration required when a student expresses concepts in writing, the resultant benefit is the probability of deeper learning. The *Standards* indicate that more emphasis must be made to integrate writing activities into the planning of math instruction.

During the past two decades, students have been trained through elementary, middle school, and high school English classrooms to view writing as a process. They have become more and more accustomed to the sequential steps of brainstorming, drafting, peer editing, polishing, and presenting their writing samples. The nature or process of writing has become clearer to students through such instruction and practice. Writing workshop structures have emphasized the repetition of process as students increase their ability to write. The awareness of the sequential nature of the writing process links nicely with the sequential processes that students need to follow in mathematics.

Researchers have also determined that students tend to remember concepts more clearly when they are asked to write about them (Postamentier & Stepelman, 1995). For example, when we ask students to explain the Pythagorean theorem, we often hear, "I know what it is. I just can't explain it." Most of us remember hearing ourselves reply, "If you can't explain it, you don't really understand it!" Providing activities in the math class that require students to write about concepts, theorems, and formulae creates opportunities for students to learn at a deeper level. Many of us have said that we've truly learned our subject area through teaching it. Having to explain what we know to other people increases the depth of our own understanding.

Writing in the math classroom can take a variety of forms and can be utilized at various times within the 90-minute block.

Index-Card Closure

An easy way to evaluate students and to gauge their level of frustration and/or confusion is to pass out index cards at the conclusion of the period. On the front, students are directed to explain what they've learned today. On the back of the card, they answer the question, "What questions remain in your mind?" This simple activity, which takes only five minutes, can reveal vital evaluative information, which we can then use to open the next class session. In addition, explaining what they've learned in writing increases the depth of students' own understanding. The index cards are easily and quickly scanned by the teacher. The teacher can even consider the questions, selecting those that can be used to introduce the next day's class.

The Informal Journal

A variation on the index-card closure is the informal journal that students keep throughout the course and into which they enter their written explanations of what they have learned and what questions remain in their minds. This format provides a more relaxed interaction between student and teacher. Periodic review of journals can reveal a great deal about students' perceptions and attitudes, as well as the correctness of their understanding of concepts covered in class. For example, when students are instructed to journal each day, providing entries that address what they understand, how they demonstrated the understanding, areas of difficulty, and why they experienced difficulty, they often reveal interesting perceptions. Table 9–9 reveals an interesting point about the logic of mathematics.

Reading these student entries is rewarding but can also be time consuming. One way to cut down on the extra time that journal reading will take is to use the same time given to students for entering information and questions in their indi-

TABLE 9–9   An Algebra II Quadratic Formula Journal Entry

I know how to plug in the variables in the quadratic formula because I could follow the examples in class and do the problems in class. Why should I go through the whole thing and come up with one set that doesn't work when I put it back into the equation?

O.K., now I get it. When my dad was going over the homework with me, he explained that the +/− in the quadratic was like a computer programming logic statement. I should read it as "plus or minus" so that the real solution will be one of those, not both. I wish my teacher would teach us why we follow these steps, not just how to follow them.

vidual journals to circulate throughout the room, scanning and initializing student pages. As long as the teacher does this in a quiet, nonthreatening, informal manner, students will not be intimidated by this observation. This strategy allows the students to know that we really are reading their journal entries. It gives us immediate feedback as they write, and it is an efficient use of class time.

The Writing Log

Setting up the structure for a writing log to be used throughout the course is a good way for students to keep track of concepts learned each day and a reinforcer for processes practiced. Postamentier and Stepelman (1995) suggest that categories be used with each entry into the student log. The student records the date, a heading that indicates the concept taught, a section for an explanation of any new relationships introduced, a new-term/definition division, crucial points to study, and a section in which the student describes whatever procedure or sequence of steps may be needed to apply the new concept. The teacher can provide this format at the beginning of the course (see Table 9–10).

This writing log can become an important resource for students as they review for tests. It also provides them with a record in their own words of all concepts and processes covered in class to date. This log can become the basis of the Think-Pair-Share cooperative learning activity discussed in Chapter 3 as well. When students compare what partners have written about new concepts, processes, and relationships, they more clearly understand material covered in class. They can also edit the work of their group members, sharpening definitions and giving more specific directions for sequential steps in procedures.

The Quick Write

The Quick Write is a useful strategy. Before homework is reviewed, a two-minute Quick Write can ask students to describe the problems causing them trouble or the problems that took the most time to solve and the reasons that that was so. If a student has had no trouble with the homework, the teacher can ask that student to provide an explanation in writing for solving one of the problems that the teacher already knows to be a source of trouble for most students. This strategy primes the students for a more active homework review. It clarifies problem areas for them to address during the review. The Quick Write also gives us valuable information

TABLE 9–10 Writing Log Structural Format

General Instructions: You are to complete entries in your Algebra I learning log throughout the course. All writing must be done in complete sentences except in the new-term/definition category.

	Categories
Section 1	Write the date and a heading that describes the new concept introduced.
Section 2	Explain in a paragraph the new concept and the importance of this concept to Algebra I.
Section 3	List all new terms and definitions in short phrases.
Section 4	Describe crucial information to be mastered; list sequential steps of the process.

about student comprehension, thus making the homework review that follows more specifically focused on problem areas. It is a more effective approach than the usual, "Are there any questions?" which may produce responses only from the truly interested student.

This same strategy is effective between activities as a mini-closure. It can be used any time but provides a short, revitalizing change of pace after a homework review, after the introduction of a new concept, or as a short explanation of procedure after a practice-problem session. Although a Quick Write may only take five minutes of class time to complete and then share with the class, it can clarify and serve to reinforce essential concepts. It also reenergizes a class after 20 to 30 minutes of lecture, practice, or review work.

Translation Time

High school students are in varying stages of cognitive development. Some handle abstractions well, while others struggle with math because they have trouble translating symbols into the processes they represent. The *Standards* emphasize the need for students to understand mathematics as it is used in everyday life. Statistics are reported by all media, leading to student exposure to symbols, graphs, and tables on a daily basis. One translation activity asks students to pick a graph from a newspaper article and explain what it describes in writing. They can enter that description into their journals on a regular basis, or they can prepare the description so that the graph and their explanation can be shared either with their small group or with the class.

The translation strategy is also helpful to make formulae more concrete and therefore more easily remembered and followed. In an elective statistics class, for example, students have to have a grasp of calculation of the mean in order to proceed to other, more involved analyses. If the students have to explain each symbol and step in the formula, they will have the opportunity to increase their understanding while reducing any anxiety level they may have about formulae in general.

The student first defines the mean and puts the symbol in parenthesis after the definition. Then, a description of the rest of the formula follows, with the student still including each symbol in parenthesis where applicable (see Table 9–11). Putting the symbolic terms into words can clear up procedures for many students.

Writing and Presenting Problems

After a concept has been introduced and practice sessions have helped students to deal with the processes of solving problems, they can be asked to apply the concept

---

TABLE 9–11 Student Translation—Journal Entry

The mean, $\overline{X}$, of our test scores is the average test score, the arithmetic middle score. The formula for finding the mean is

$$\overline{X} = \frac{\Sigma X}{N}$$

The average score ($\overline{X}$) is found by adding (Σ) each student's score (X) and dividing that answer by the number of scores (N). 20 of us took the 30-point test so N equals 20. All of our scores add up to 575. If I divide 575 by 20, I get an average score of 28.75 points. So the mean is 28.75. We did great!

---

to a real-life situation from their own experience by creating a problem for the other students to solve. The problem cannot be a simple substitution of numbers from one of the problems already done in class. Each student creates a problem, writes an explanation for the use of this concept in real life, and describes the procedure used to solve the problem. The students then present the problem to their small group or to the whole class to solve. An alternative approach includes the teacher's request that all students submit the above for approval before any problems are presented to the class. The teacher then picks the student-created problems most useful for everyone to do. The next day's class begins with several students presenting their problems for others to solve. Listening to the presentations of these problems gives the teacher an opportunity to evaluate the depth of student understanding.

Writing Directions

A good way to help students develop the ability to give precise explanations is to have them write a process in a letter to a friend who has missed a lesson on calculating probability, for example. Hypothetically, the student's friend will pass or fail on the basis of his ability to follow the directions for solving a problem based on the written directions in the letter.

In addition, students can use this strategy to analyze exact procedures needed to create a geometric figure. Without naming the type of figure, the student must describe the process so clearly that his or her partner can read the directions and create the figure exactly as it should be constructed. If the students are paired, each tries to construct a figure based on the written directions of his partner.

Word Bank Review

Reviews can be a good opportunity for students to write. If we give them a list of terms used in describing a concept and the procedure for solving problems using this concept, their task is to use all terms in a written explanation of the concept and sequence of steps for solving a sample problem. For example, in consumer math, we could give the following scenario:

> After school yesterday, I went to the bank and deposited $200 that I earned by refereeing this season's basketball games. The bank teller told me that I could earn interest if I put the money in a savings account. She said it would be a fixed rate of 4% and it would be compounded annually. If I leave it in the account until this class graduates from high school in two years, how much money will I have?

The teacher puts a word bank on the board (Table 9–12). The word bank includes terms listed in random order that the students might include in their clearly sequenced written explanation. It could also include symbols needed to solve the problem.

TABLE 9–12 Word Bank for Consumer Math

interest rate	number of years
accumulated amount	equation
compounded	fixed
initial deposit	

Directions: Using the words above, explain how you would solve my problem.

FURTHER CONSIDERATIONS AND OPTIONS

Administrators and teachers might wish to research, consider, and discuss the scheduling of math classes in a variety of ways that may deviate from the usual 90-minute class meeting every day for a semester or meeting every other day for the whole school year. For example, if a school district has concerns about Algebra I coverage in one semester, they may consider splitting one 90-minute block so that students attend Algebra I all year for 45 minutes each day and then take two other traditionally semester-long courses during the other 45-minute part of the block. For example, students might take Algebra I in the first half of the 90-minute block and then take Health in the second half for the first semester; during the second semester the ninth graders would stay with Algebra I but then take Physical Education in the second half of the block. The other three 90-minute blocks of their schedule would not be affected by such an arrangement. Rettig and Canady (1998) suggest that a course as crucial as Algebra I be divided into four parts, with concept mastery evaluated after each part. Such a configuration might utilize two semesters of 90-minute block or "a daily block within the A/B schedule" so that teachers can accommodate "variable learning time" (p. 57).

Other suggestions for the teaching of mathematics include the following:

- The creation of a two-part algebra class for lower level mathematics students
- The replacement of the normal first-year/second-year algebra sequence with a sequence of three shorter algebra courses
- The modification of geometry and first-year algebra courses to eliminate topics taught in second-year algebra
- The creation of two separate classes to replace a combined second-year algebra and trigonometry class
- The addition of new courses, such as statistics, for students who complete the regular sequence. (Kramer, 1996, p. 760)

The student beginning the block schedule as a junior and just beginning geometry at the same time may be at a disadvantage in preparing to take the college boards. Controversy continues to revolve around the standardized test achievement of students on extended-block schedules. Additionally, Advanced Placement courses need to be considered carefully by mathematics teachers planning for the block. Kramer (1996) notes: "In some cases, schools using block schedules offer calculus and other AP courses as double-length courses that run the entire year . . . or three quarters of the year . . . with the last quarter perhaps offering a class on a special topic, such as probability or statistics" (p. 761).

The timing of the AP exams becomes an issue of concern for teachers on the block. As of September 1996, the College Board had received numerous requests for the scheduling of AP exams in January and the postponement of the current exam schedule until later in May or in June. The May examination schedule will be one week later, beginning in May 1998. The January exam request is still being studied, with no change predicted soon because the projected number of students who would be taking the January exam in 1999 is currently too small to warrant a change.

Teaching mathematics in the extended block does present challenges, but many options, like those listed here, can alleviate concerns and also address achievement as measured on standardized tests. Moreover, to make optimum use of the extended period provided by the block, the math teacher needs to incorporate many participatory activities into daily lessons. As mathematics teachers, we can take advantage of this extended time to draw on our own knowledge of subject matter and instructional skills in order to rethink and revitalize our teaching. Integrating student-active approaches like cooperative learning, inquiry-based lessons, collaborative strategies, real-world scenarios, experiments, and writing applications can increase student motivation and deepen learning. Extra planning time allows us to investigate stronger interdisciplinary activities so that our students can practice their mathematics in the context of other subjects as well as in their math classes. Instead of dreading the change from the traditional 50-minute class period to the extended block, we can welcome the flexibility and increased options it gives us to effectively teach mathematics.

FIGURE 9–1   Planning in Chunks of Time: Building an Integrated Math Plan

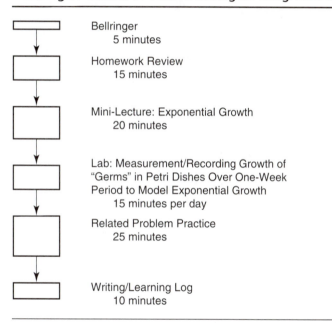

Bellringer
5 minutes

Homework Review
15 minutes

Mini-Lecture: Exponential Growth
20 minutes

Lab: Measurement/Recording Growth of "Germs" in Petri Dishes Over One-Week Period to Model Exponential Growth
15 minutes per day

Related Problem Practice
25 minutes

Writing/Learning Log
10 minutes

TABLE 9–13 Putting Your Thoughts in Order: Mathematics

1. List the most important concepts/skills that you want your students to understand/master before they walk out of your room at the end of the course.
2. List effective activities now used to address each goal.
3. Indicate which concepts/skills you wish to address in more depth.
4. Think of ways in which you can contextualize each goal with reality-based activities.
5. Consider various strategies that you might add to address each goal: cooperative learning, inquiry learning, study skill strategies, inclusion of computer applications and other technology, use of manipulatives. List them for each goal.

Goals	1. Concept Skills	2. Content Selections	3. Current Activities	4. More Depth	5. Personalize, Contextualize	6. New Ideas
1.						
2.						
3.						
4.						
5.						
6.						
7.						
8.						
9.						
10.						

■ PART THREE
Suggestions
from Colleagues

An integrated approach to instruction allows students to look at an issue from multiple viewpoints.

Planning for the extended block becomes easier when we have access to examples. In this section, several sample plans give direction to those of us just beginning to think of lessons as 90-minute units. Practicing teachers, student teachers, and advanced undergraduate education majors preparing to teach in extended-block schools present plans that they have created in several secondary subject areas and that are applicable to a variety of block configurations. These examples include the following:

Objectives
Activities
Approximate minutes needed to accomplish each

They combine traditional approaches such as the mini-lecture, whole-class discussion, and guided practice with more contemporary approaches including cooperative learning, integrated curricula, inquiry learning, writing across the curriculum, and the integration of various subject-area concepts as they complement and enhance the goals of each course.

We are grateful to those colleagues who have graciously shared their ideas with us and trust that the samples will be useful to all secondary school professionals considering a move to the extended-block schedule.

■ ALGEBRA I

James Waychoff
Mathematics Education
Edinboro University of PA
Edinboro, PA

LINEAR EQUATIONS

TYPE OF EXTENDED BLOCK 4×4
NUMBER OF MINUTES PER CLASS   85

OBJECTIVES   The student will:

1. write the equation of a line using 2 points, a point and a line, a point and an implied slope;

2. graph the equation of the line;

3. determine the x and y intercepts of a line using an equation.

ACTIVITY 1   The teacher instructs the students to use graph paper to draw a line, hypothesize methods to determine slope. Discussion of methods used. | 10 minutes

ACTIVITY 2   Mini-lecture—introduction to writing equations of lines in Standard and Slope-Intercept forms and explanation of using the point–slope formula. Students take notes. | 10 minutes

ACTIVITY 3   The teacher models the steps for two examples while the students give him step-by-step directions; three students do examples as the class directs each of them. | 20 minutes

ACTIVITY 4   Mini-lecture—explanation of procedure for finding intercepts of previous equations where the other variable = 0 and then solving for the first variable. The Standard form and the Slope-Intercept form are demonstrated. Students take notes. | 10 minutes

ACTIVITY 5   The teacher demonstrates with a new example as the students give directions. Two students then demonstrate while the class directs them. | 15 minutes

ACTIVITY 6   Informal journal review—students write responses to questions posed by the teacher. What do we need to write the equation of a line? What is the point–slope formula? What do m and b represent in the equation of a line? The teacher continues to pose questions. After responses have been written, students pair with a partner to compare responses. The teacher then asks for the responses in a whole-class review. | 20 minutes

■ ALGEBRA II

Jana Baxter
Mathematics Education
Edinboro University of PA

QUADRATIC EQUATIONS

ACADEMIC LEVEL Average, Above average
TYPE OF EXTENDED BLOCK 4×4
NUMBER OF MINUTES PER CLASS 80

OBJECTIVES The student will:

1. recall the standard form of the quadratic equation;

2. model the procedure for completing the square on the standard form of the quadratic equation;

3. produce the quadratic formula via Objective 2;

4. justify reasons for procedural steps in the production of the quadratic formula;

5. list three possible solution methods for solving the quadratic equation.

ACTIVITY 1 Homework review of completing the square to solve a quadratic equation. 10 minutes

ACTIVITY 2 Think-Pair-Share—Two quadratic equations to solve using the completing-the-square method. 10 minutes

ACTIVITY 3 Discussion: What is the standard form of the quadratic equation? Referring to the previous equation, what corresponds to a, b, and c in the standard form? 10 minutes

ACTIVITY 4 Students work independently on worksheet to solve the standard form of the quadratic equation by completing the square. Teacher will answer questions with only yes or no and then write questions/responses on the board for all to see. 25 minutes

ACTIVITY 5 What is the solution for x? What is the solution called? This might take awhile for students to give the right response (the quadratic formula). 15 minutes

ACTIVITY 6 Give the students a quadratic equation and have them solve it using the quadratic formula. 5 minutes

ACTIVITY 7 Closure. We now know of three possible ways to solve a quadratic equation. What are they? (factoring, completing the square, quadratic formula). Assign homework. 5 minutes

BIOLOGY

Karen Yonko
Conneaut Lake High School
Conneaut Lake, PA

ANIMAL KINGDOMS

GRADE LEVEL   10
NUMBER OF MINUTES PER CLASS   85

OBJECTIVES   The student will:

1. define the following terms: *eukaryote, multicellular, unicellular, autotroph, heterotroph;*

2. list the five kingdom names, a minimum of five vocabulary terms to describe each, and an example of an organism in each kingdom;

3. design and present a poster that is divided into five sections (one for each kingdom);

4. listen attentively during a poster presentation.

ACTIVITY 1	Ask the students to list five kingdoms orally. Write the vocabulary words on the board and have the students define. After defining, discuss terms.	15 minutes
ACTIVITY 2	Give notes on the five kingdoms and the vocabulary words that describe them. Also give one example of each. Ask the students for input and other examples.	15 minutes
ACTIVITY 3	Instruct the students to construct a poster. The students must then use a minimum of three vocabulary words to describe. For example, *unicellular* (draw a picture of a cell phone), *multicellular* (draw more than one cell phone). Let the students decide the symbols. They must use the same symbol each time it appears on the poster.	25 minutes
ACTIVITY 4	Let the students present the posters to the class.	15 minutes
ACTIVITY 5	Give the students a quiz on the five kingdoms using the vocabulary that describes them. Let the students look at their posters to see if they can remember the proper vocabulary terms.	5 minutes

■ CALCULUS

Judy Scaletta
General McLane High School
Edinboro, PA

AP CALCULUS: THE DECAY PROCESS

TYPE OF EXTENDED BLOCK 4×4
NUMBER OF MINUTES PER CLASS   85

OBJECTIVES   The student will:

1. simulate the decay process and construct mathematical models;

2. construct a natural exponential function to model the decay process;

3. develop a definition of *half-life*.

ACTIVITY 1   Cooperative Learning   5 minutes
Unit Objectives Review: Review card
Students are given a note card with a review problem to
complete and explain. Students work with a partner.

ACTIVITY 2   Homework Review   12 minutes
Cover Homework
Students put yesterday's problems on the board and explain
them to the class.

ACTIVITY 3   Mini-Lecture   15 minutes
Introduction to Exponential Decay
Lecture by teacher. Guided practice problems.
Students refer to the AIDS simulation from Unit I; the growth
pattern was an exponential function.
Questions: What is the form of the equation produced by an
exponential regression on the calculator? List some of the
characteristics of our model.
Discuss two exponential models to be used today.

ACTIVITY 4   Laboratory: Modeling exponential decay with marbles and dice.   50 minutes
Distribute lab sheets; have students read directions; check for
understanding.
Demonstrate the proper use of the marble sifters. Allow 45
minutes to collect the data for the labs.
(*Note:* Each person must write his or her own lab report.)

ACTIVITY 5   Closure and Assignment   5 minutes
What difficulties did you have collecting data?
What is your group's definition of half-life?
How could you construct a natural exponential model for each
data set?
Finish the analysis questions for tomorrow.

■ CAREER PLANNING

Elizabeth Legler
North East High School
North East, PA

CAREER CHOICES

GRADE LEVEL 9
TYPE OF EXTENDED BLOCK A/B trimester
NUMBER OF MINUTES PER CLASS 90

OBJECTIVES The student will:

1. receive a realistic view of how financial considerations will be important when deciding on a career path;

2. have the opportunity to gain poise and confidence in front of peers.

ACTIVITY 1 Bellringer—Description of various jobs mounted on cards. As students enter the room every day, they take a card from the box, read it, and write a one-paragraph description in their journal. (What they found interesting, facts they didn't know before, why they would or would not follow the career).   10 minutes

ACTIVITY 2 Students do a budget profile. Information including prices is included in folders for every category in the budget. Students are given a lifestyle—single, married, single with children, or married with children. Students get information from folders and using calculators, determine a budget for their assigned lifestyle. This budget would be for them at age 29.   80 minutes

ACTIVITY 3 After the budget is checked and corrected by the teacher, students mount rewritten, revised budget on poster and create a collage of pictures describing their budget.   90 minutes

ACTIVITY 4 Students present their lifestyle and budget to the class.

■ CHILD DEVELOPMENT

Elizabeth Legler
North East High School
North East, PA

PLANNING FOR A BABY

GRADE LEVEL 9–12
TYPE OF EXTENDED BLOCK A/B trimester
NUMBER OF MINUTES PER CLASS 90

OBJECTIVES   The student will:

1. understand proper techniques when diapering and bathing a newborn and a toddler;

2. recognize safety hazards in a bathroom;

3. comprehend the costs involved in setting up a nursery.

ACTIVITY 1   Lecture and discussion: Safety in the home with babies.   10 minutes

ACTIVITY 2   Demonstration: Bathing and diapering a newborn and toddler   20 minutes
(using dolls, baby tub, bathing and diapering supplies).

ACTIVITY 3   Teacher lays out approximately 35–50 nursery and baby items   60 minutes
with price tags on them. Discussion of the cost of items that will
be needed to set up a nursery will follow. (Prices are put on
pictures of larger items—e.g., cribs, playpens, walkers, high
chairs.)

ACTIVITY 4   Using the budget form supplied by the teacher, students walk
around the tables and determine number of each item they want and
prices. Students add up the amount of money needed to set up
a nursery. The teacher puts no price limit on this. Students find
out how costly it is to have a baby.

■ ECOLOGY

Karen Yonko
Conneaut Lake High School
Conneaut Lake, PA

ENDANGERED SPECIES

GRADE LEVEL 11–12
NUMBER OF MINUTES PER CLASS 85

OBJECTIVES The student will:

1. read individual handouts of PA endangered species (you could have them research first if you have more time);

2. work in groups of four to orally describe their PA endangered species and have them collectively choose one species to save;

3. design a platform to save one species and create a slogan and poster to convince the class to save their species;

4. listen attentively and respectfully during each platform and vote for one species to save for the entire class.

Day 1

ACTIVITY 1 Have the students recall orally the definition for *endangered species*. Brainstorm some endangered species in PA. Pass out PA endangered species handouts (or begin research). Have the students read about their endangered species. **15 minutes**

ACTIVITY 2 Break the students into groups of four. Tell each group member to first describe their species, then have the group decide which species they want to save. **15 minutes**

ACTIVITY 3 Tell the students they must come up with a group platform to save the group species. The platform must have a catchy slogan and a poster. They must come up with political, economical, ecological, social, and personal reasons for saving their species. The reasons must be clearly stated on the poster along with the slogan. **35 minutes**

ACTIVITY 4 The students must then present their platforms to the class. The class will then vote on the species they would like to save based on the platforms. **20 minutes**

Day 2

ACTIVITY 5 Ask the students for ideas on saving the endangered species. What is the best way to save endangered species? Introduce the concept of habitat preservation. Ask the students why it is important to try to save the endangered species. **20–30 minutes**

■ ECONOMICS

Neil Milligan
General McLane High School
Edinboro, PA

STARTING A NEW BUSINESS

TYPE OF EXTENDED BLOCK 4×4
GRADE LEVEL   11–12
NUMBER OF MINUTES PER CLASS   85

OBJECTIVES   The students will:

1. analyze their own potential to be a future businessperson;

2. brainstorm ideas to create their own business and evaluate what idea suits them or their partners best;

3. discover available library information to answer questions involving entrepreneurship.

ACTIVITY 1	Bellringer—students must state a business that they would like to operate.	5 minutes
ACTIVITY 2	Mini-lecture using overheads—the teacher shows and explains "Guidelines for Starting a New Business."	15 minutes
ACTIVITY 3	Guest speaker—outside businessperson who explains how he or she started, the pitfalls, surprises, etc., and answers student questions.	20 minutes
ACTIVITY 4	Cooperative learning—groups of three list five positive and five negative personal traits. Students create further ideas for a potential summer business (individual or partnership).	20 minutes
ACTIVITY 5	Students report to the library with a source list provided to find information to assist in setting up a business/answer questions from brainstorming session.	20 minutes
ACTIVITY 6	Closure—guided discussion led by students. Students create more questions about information they need/want about setting up a business.	5 minutes

■ ENGLISH

Denise Graham
Student Teacher
Edinboro University of PA

LITERATURE, HISTORY, MUSIC OF THE '20S AND '30S

GRADE LEVEL   10
TYPE OF EXTENDED BLOCK 4×4
NUMBER OF MINUTES PER CLASS   85

OBJECTIVES   The student will:

1. recognize various 1930s composers and their work;

2. characterize regionalism and social consciousness as it applies to music of the '30s;

3. compare and contrast music of the '20s and '30s;

4. identify national issues that influenced music of the '30s.

ACTIVITY 1   In a quick-write, students will offer predictions about the music of the '20s and '30s.   2 minutes

ACTIVITY 2   Students will visit four learning stations set up in the room. At each station, they will be required to answer several questions based on auditory/visual experience. Four stations are as follows: 35 minutes

Station 1: Radio recording of Will Rogers commenting on FDR
Station 2: 8-min. video clip of Gershwin's opera, *Porgy and Bess*
Station 3: Recording of 1930s swing music (vernacular)
Station 4: Recording of Copland's *Billy the Kid* (cultivated)

Each group of four students will have eight minutes at each station to listen and answer questions. Teacher will monitor.

ACTIVITY 3   Students will discuss each station and musical experience, identify regionalism, social consciousness, artist, and overall influence of the time period (small-group discussion).   20 minutes

ACTIVITY 4   Whole-group debriefing emphasizing regionalism, social consciousness, national issues.   25 minutes

ACTIVITY 5   Students will be asked to identify a contemporary artist, either vernacular or cultivated, who displays regionalism or social consciousness and to validate their choices through explanation.   3 minutes

■ ENGLISH

Karen Kelmickis
English Education
Edinboro University of PA

POE'S "FALL OF THE HOUSE OF USHER"

GRADE LEVEL 11
TYPE OF EXTENDED BLOCK 4×4
NUMBER OF MINUTES PER CLASS 90

OBJECTIVES The student will:

1. define a select group of words from "The Fall of the House of Usher";

2. summarize the story;

3. support themes, ideas, concepts in the story.

ACTIVITY 1 Vocabulary lesson—Students work in pairs to complete chart consisting of each word, student prediction of its meaning, and definition gathered from context clues. (Handouts—2) 40 minutes

ACTIVITY 2 Quick Draw—Students draw a picture of the house as described by Poe. 10 minutes

ACTIVITY 3 Teacher explains the trial simulation and divides the class, describing jobs of the prosecution, defense, and jury. Students will be placed on a team. They will be given a case from the story to prosecute, defend, or judge. (Handout) 10 minutes

ACTIVITY 4 This activity will continue into the next day's class. Simulation trial—Students present their side of the case. Students are evaluated on their presentation of the facts and examples, not on whether they win or lose. 75 minutes

Simulation trial concept from M. Britt, *Research on Trial: A Pedagogy for Research Methods Instruction* (Poughkeepsie, NY: Marist College).

■ ENGLISH

Candice Kemp
General McLane High School
Edinboro, PA

THE MYSTERY NOVEL

TYPE OF EXTENDED BLOCK 4×4
NUMBER OF MINUTES PER CLASS   85

OBJECTIVES   The student will:

1. construct sentences using daily vocabulary and assigned grammar function correctly;

2. report orally his or her summary of outside reading of mystery novels, identifying any rising action;

3. list information found in fellow students' summaries.

ACTIVITY 1   Guided Practice   10 minutes

After teacher has posted the Word of the Day and has assigned a grammar function for that word, students will go to posting area, copy information on worksheet, and write a sentence. Teacher will roam classroom editing student work. Peer editing is an option.

ACTIVITY 2   Cooperative Learning   30 minutes

Students will form their small discussion groups; rotating facilitator will call for reporting summaries. Students may question each other as to plot line. At the end of reading seminar session, students will predict outcome for each other's mystery novels. Additionally, students will list rising action from each novel presented.

ACTIVITY 3   Guided Reading   30 minutes

Teacher will read aloud a short mystery story from textbook, setting tone and pace. Teacher will call on one student to help in oral reading, and, in turn, this student will call on another, and so on until story is complete.

ACTIVITY 4   Guided Practice   15 minutes

Students will complete reading exercises for story and will complete one block of their eight-block storyboard of the Sherlock Holmes mystery read previously.

■ ENGLISH

Candice Kemp
General McLane High School
Edinboro, PA

AMERICAN LITERATURE: EMILY DICKINSON

TYPE OF EXTENDED BLOCK 4×4
NUMBER OF MINUTES PER CLASS   85

OBJECTIVES   The student will:

1. state influencing facts on Emily Dickinson's life and her style characteristics;

2. apply style characteristics of Emily Dickinson to her poetry, giving examples.

ACTIVITY 1   Mini-lecture   25 minutes

Students will take notes on the life and style of Emily Dickinson while teacher lectures. Students will observe teacher explicate the poem "Some Keep the Sabbath Going to Church," asking any questions needed.

ACTIVITY 2   Guided Practice/Cooperative Learning   25 minutes

Students will explicate in groups of four an assigned Dickinson poem, recording results. Teacher will visit each group, giving assistance if needed. After explication exercise, teacher will provide answer sheet to each group.

ACTIVITY 3   Guided Practice/Cooperative Learning   25 minutes

Two members of original group will rotate to a new group of remaining two. This newly formed group will explicate a new poem, following the previous procedure. Teacher will visit groups, monitoring progress. Answer sheet will be provided again.

ACTIVITY 4   Closure   5 minutes

Students will fill out "Exit Slips" indicating understanding of Emily Dickinson's style or confusion. Teacher will begin lesson tomorrow based on this information. Allow 5 to 10 minutes at the beginning of tomorrow's class.

Keith Miller
English Education
Edinboro University of PA

CREATIVE WRITING

GRADE LEVEL 9
ACADEMIC LEVEL Heterogeneous
NUMBER OF MINUTES PER CLASS 85

OBJECTIVES The student will:

1. develop a hypothesis concerning description through participation in sensory provoking activities;

2. identify the form and function of a description;

3. apply knowledge of descriptors to a spontaneous written assignment;

4. practice oral presentation skills.

ACTIVITY 1 Show the students a delicious looking piece of double chocolate cake and have them tell you what they see. Now, pass out a piece of the cake to each student, have them taste the cake, and then do a focused writing on what was tasted.   10 minutes

ACTIVITY 2 Students will read a passage of text (individually) that is loaded with very rich descriptive terms and they will underline whatever they feel is important. Students will then pair together to answer two questions: (1) Why did we underline the words that we did? (2) What might we call these terms?   20 minutes

ACTIVITY 3 Teacher asks the pairs to contribute their answers to these questions and writes a synopsis of these contributions on the board. The teacher will use this to begin a guided discussion of descriptors and their relevance to writing creatively.   20 minutes

ACTIVITY 4 Teacher distributes a peanut (with shell) and has students write a description of the object.   10 minutes

ACTIVITY 5 Students will then share, through oral presentations, their descriptive writing of the peanut.   20 minutes

■ ENGLISH

Keith Miller
English Education
Edinboro University of PA

CREATIVE WRITING AND POINT OF VIEW

GRADE LEVEL 9–10
NUMBER OF MINUTES PER CLASS 85

OBJECTIVES The student will:

1. offer a hypothesis on point of view based on the reading of three excerpts depicting differing points of view;

2. acquire information concerning the advantages and limitations of each point of view through participation in a guided discussion;

3. apply understanding of point of view by rewriting previous assignment in a different point of view.

ACTIVITY 1 The teacher will have students read three prepared stories, each depicting a different point of view (first, third full omniscient, second limited omniscient). Students will pair together to compare/contrast the three stories (2–3 paragraphs each). The students will write their analysis on a piece of paper (hypothesis). 20 minutes

ACTIVITY 2 Each group then presents these findings to the rest of the class and the teacher writes a synopsis on the board. A guided discussion follows as the teacher leads the students to the three point-of-view forms mentioned in Activity 1. 20 minutes

ACTIVITY 3 Present a handout (or show transparency) of the definitions of the three points of view. Read a passage(s) from a story that is obviously enhanced by its point of view (like Poe's "Tell Tale Heart"), and discuss possible advantages that the author is attaining. 10 minutes

ACTIVITY 4 Student will choose a story that they previously wrote, change the point of view, and rewrite it. 15 minutes

ACTIVITY 5 Students will break into groups of four or five to read one another's original story and then the revised point of view. Students will offer feedback to each other concerning the accuracy of their point-of-view revisions. 20 minutes

■ ENGLISH

Deborah Nauman
English Education
Edinboro University of PA

ELEMENTS OF A STORY

GRADE LEVEL 9
NUMBER OF MINUTES PER CLASS 90

OBJECTIVES The student will:

1. demonstrate knowledge of elements of a story;

2. make predictions;

3. apply the story's theme of women's roles in society;

4. demonstrate comprehension of assigned vocabulary words;

5. improve listening, writing, reading, and speaking skills.

ACTIVITY 1 Learning station. Vocabulary/point of view. Highlight vocabulary in first page of "An Upheaval" by Anton Chekhov. Look up meaning and part of speech in dictionary. Roundrobin exercise to rewrite scene from point of view of another character. 20 minutes

ACTIVITY 2 Learning station. Plot/Character. Individual and group predictions based on textual support. Group must come to a consensus on predictions. 20 minutes

ACTIVITY 3 Learning station. Setting. Group answers questions regarding description effect of setting. Responses are a group consensus and based on textual support. Each member draws a picture of the setting to convey mood and physical environment. 20 minutes

ACTIVITY 4 Learning station. Plot/character. Students convey emotion written on cards using his or her face only. Group determines plot and composes stage directions. Group records dialogue on tape recorder and mimes first scene to student-generated dialogue. 20 minutes

ACTIVITY 5 Sponge activity. Journal entry. Compare/contrast women's roles in society when story was written to women's roles today. 10 minutes

■ ENGLISH

Deborah Nauman
English Education
Edinboro University of PA

THE SHORT STORY

GRADE LEVEL 9
TYPE OF EXTENDED BLOCK 4 × 4
NUMBER OF MINUTES PER CLASS 90

OBJECTIVES The student will:

1. demonstrate knowledge and effect of setting;

2. express opinions of the characters' behavior;

3. improve comprehension skills;

4. improve analytical abilities;

5. apply the story's theme of learning from mistakes.

ACTIVITY 1	Anticipation Guide. Cooperative learning groups. Individual and group consensus of guide. Responses recorded on the overhead.	20 minutes
ACTIVITY 2	Silent in-class reading of "The Man of the House."	20 minutes
ACTIVITY 3	Cooperative learning groups. Students compare their responses to the anticipation guide with the author's. There must be a group consensus and textual support for responses. Responses are shared with the class.	20 minutes
ACTIVITY 4	Cooperative learning groups. Students compare/contrast settings of "The Garden Party" and "Man of the House" and their effect on the stories. Students complete questions on the handout.	20 minutes
ACTIVITY 5	Grammar activity. Identify the subject/object distinctions in the first two paragraphs of "The Man of the House." Students circle the subjects and box the objects in each sentence to use as examples while reviewing the grammatical rules. The teacher passes out pictures of nouns, and each student composes two sentences using the item shown on the noun flashcard. One sentence shows the noun as a subject and the other shows the noun as the object of a sentence. The teacher selects sentences for display on the overhead. Students circle the subjects and objects.	20 minutes

■ ENGLISH

Donald Plyler
English Education
Edinboro University of PA

NOTE TAKING

GRADE LEVEL 8
ACADEMIC LEVEL Heterogeneous
NUMBER OF MINUTES PER CLASS 90

OBJECTIVES The students will:

1. define paraphrasing in their own words after participating in an anticipatory set;

2. practice using note-taking techniques by participating in a writing-station activity;

3. identify the proper note-taking method by reviewing the correct ways to use note cards.

Day 1

ACTIVITY 1 Read aloud the paragraph written on the overhead. Together with the class, paraphrase the paragraph.   15 minutes

ACTIVITY 2 The students will go through three of the six stations paraphrasing each paragraph. They will have 10 minutes for each station. Then we will go over each group's work, and the students will receive handouts on paraphrasing.   50 minutes

Day 2

ACTIVITY 3 Start with a mini-lesson on how to construct note cards properly. The students will then rewrite the paragraph from the first activity. They will need to paraphrase the paragraph into four or five sentences and write a bibliography citation.   15 minutes

ACTIVITY 4 At this point, the students will have time to go back through as many stations as possible and practice. After 40 minutes, the entire class will go to the library to continue research for 30 minutes.   70 minutes

■ ENGLISH

April Watkins
English Education
Edinboro University of PA

AMERICAN POETRY

GRADE LEVEL 9
ACADEMIC LEVEL Basic English
NUMBER OF MINUTES PER CLASS 90

OBJECTIVES The student will:

1. display an interest in poetry by being actively involved in the discussion of poetry;

2. develop appreciation for "Democracy" and "Still I Rise" by reading them silently and orally;

3. discover the themes of the poems "Democracy" and "Still I Rise" through Phase One of a learning cycle;

4. evaluate the themes of the poems and learn new concepts through Phase Two of a learning cycle;

5. create poem using concepts through Phase Three of a learning cycle;

6. actively listen to mini-lectures on the concepts of poetry.

ACTIVITY 1	Students recap poems in Langston Hughes. Introduce Maya Angelou, give some background information on her, and discuss some of her poetry.	10 minutes
ACTIVITY 2	Hand out two poems by Maya Angelou and Langston Hughes. Students will read them orally. Students will get into groups for fifteen minutes and write down everything that is similar and different in the poems. Students will discuss the similarities and differences they found.	25 minutes
ACTIVITY 3	Introduce students to new concepts: *scansion, personification,* and *onomatopoeia.* Use transparencies of the two poems "Democracy" and "Still I Rise" as visuals and help explain their use in the poem. Students will discuss the themes of the poems.	25 minutes
ACTIVITY 4	Students will have the remainder of the period to create their own poem. The poem should be an eight-line poem with at least two rhyming lines. They must use adjectives to describe themselves or an object. They must use the concepts learned in Phase Two. I will put them on the board. They will also come to me for questions they may have. I also gave them examples of the types of poem I wanted.	30 minutes

■ ENGLISH

Carla Worthen
East High School
Erie, PA

PERSONAL ESSAY

GRADE LEVEL 9
TYPE OF EXTENDED BLOCK 4 × 4
NUMBER OF MINUTES PER CLASS 80

OBJECTIVES The student will:

1. understand the eight types of personal essays by taking notes on mini-lecture with 80 percent accuracy;

2. activate schema by working in cooperative groups to write descriptive essays with 80 percent accuracy;

3. develop the ability to "show, don't tell" by a Quick Write to synthesize ideas using the five senses to write descriptive essays in class with 90 percent accuracy.

ACTIVITY 1 Mini-lecture explaining the eight types of personal essays (description, narration, how-to, comparison and contrast, definition, cause/effect, argument and persuasion). Explain that writing can be fun: "You can write about anything you want. There is only one limitation: profanity. First we are going to play a few writing games" (Bender, p. 4).   *15 minutes*

ACTIVITY 2 Groups of three or four students use the five senses written on the board and a picture on the overhead to describe what they see. (Play two games.) Give points to the most descriptive essay. Two minutes to Quick Write and one minute to share in each group.   *15 minutes*

ACTIVITY 3 Students work individually to Quick Write using the five senses and overhead picture sample. Students then describe someone they love or hate (sparking strong emotion). Do three two-minute Quick Writes. Six minutes to Quick Write and ten minutes to share (Bender, p. 15).   *16 minutes*

ACTIVITY 4 Students take notes on a four-minute mini-lecture. Remind students that using "I" is permitted and that revisions will be used to clean up the I's.   *4 minutes*

ACTIVITY 5 Show students two samples of a descriptive essay. Have students point out the sensory details in each.   *10 minutes*

ACTIVITY 6 Students choose one of their Quick Writes to develop.   *20 minutes*

CLOSURE Ask students questions pertaining to today's lesson.

SOURCES Sebranek, Meyer, & Kemper. *Writers Inc.* (Boston: Houghton Mifflin, 1996).
Bender, S. "Writing Personal Essays: How to Shape Your Life's Experience for the Page." *Writer's Digest Books*, 1995.

■ FAMILY AND CONSUMER SCIENCE

Jeanne Lamb
North East High School
North East, PA

FOODS 3: MENU PLANNING

GRADE LEVEL 11–12
TYPE OF EXTENDED BLOCK A/B trimester
NUMBER OF MINUTES PER CLASS 88

OBJECTIVES The student will:

1. show an understanding of how menu parts fit together and understand procedures for recipe preparation;

2. complete all initial preparation for the meal.

ACTIVITY 1 Teacher will review all recipes for student-planned meal plan.   10 minutes

ACTIVITY 2 *Lab:* Students will complete all first-day preparation for the Italian meal. If there is time remaining following preparation (lab.)—always have an ongoing assignment that the students can work on! This class requires a research project on the culture and cuisine of a country selected by the student.   75 minutes

Preparing and serving a meal in this class generally takes two class periods plus a previous class period to develop the meal plan.

■ FAMILY AND CONSUMER SCIENCE

Jeanne Lamb
North East High School
North East, PA

FOOD PREPARATION: RESTAURANT PROJECT

GRADE LEVEL   10–12
TYPE OF EXTENDED BLOCK   A/B trimester
NUMBER OF MINUTES PER CLASS   88

OBJECTIVES   The student will:

1. show understanding of the development of a restaurant menu;

2. begin group work on restaurant projects.

ACTIVITY 1   Review previous lesson on types of menus and how to develop a restaurant.   10 minutes

ACTIVITY 2   Introduce restaurant project and go over all instructions.   5 minutes

ACTIVITY 3   Select groups and work on project and presentations.   73 minutes

Note: This lesson is completed in one more class, followed by one-half class for oral presentations. Restaurant project instructions and rubric for evaluation of project are utilized for this plan.

■ FAMILY AND CONSUMER SCIENCE

Jeanne Lamb
North East High School
North East, PA

FOOD PREPARATION: SAFETY AND MEASURING EQUIPMENT

GRADE LEVEL 10–12
ACADEMIC LEVEL Mixed
TYPE OF EXTENDED BLOCK A/B Trimester
NUMBER OF MINUTES PER CLASS 88

OBJECTIVES The student will:

1. review safety and sanitation in the kitchen;

2. identify and properly use measuring equipment;

3. demonstrate use of measuring equipment.

ACTIVITY 1 Review previous lesson in kitchen safety and sanitation; include video "I Thought It Would Last Forever." 15 minutes

ACTIVITY 2 Lecture—types of ingredients and how to measure each. Include equivalents. 20 minutes

ACTIVITY 3 Student demonstration—chocolate chip snack cake. Students volunteer to demonstrate measuring ingredients; class critiques procedure. 35 minutes

ACTIVITY 4 Students select their cooking groups and complete a worksheet on recipe terms. 18 minutes

■ FAMILY AND CONSUMER SCIENCE

Jeanne Lamb
North East High School
North East, PA

FOOD PREPARATION: ITALIAN CUISINE

GRADE LEVEL 11–12
TYPE OF EXTENDED BLOCK A/B trimester
NUMBER OF MINUTES PER CLASS 88

OBJECTIVES The student will:

1. recognize common ingredients used in Italian cooking;

2. be able to describe the characteristics of Italian cuisine;

3. understand Italy's contribution to American cooking.

ACTIVITY 1	Using sight and smell, identify herbs used in Italian cooking. Review notes from previous day.	15 minutes
ACTIVITY 2	Filmstrip—"Italian Cooking"	15 minutes
ACTIVITY 3	Mini-lecture—completing notes on Italian cuisine.	10 minutes
ACTIVITY 4	Demonstration—samples of some common ingredients used in Italian cooking.	20 minutes
ACTIVITY 5	Mini-lecture—the order of the meal.	10 minutes
ACTIVITY 6	Students—worksheets: "What do you know about Italian cooking?" Word search—Italian foods.	18 minutes

■ FAMILY AND CONSUMER SCIENCE

Jeanne Lamb
North East High School
North East, PA

INDEPENDENT LIVING: EMPLOYMENT

GRADE LEVEL 12
TYPE OF EXTENDED BLOCK A/B trimester
NUMBER OF MINUTES PER CLASS 88

OBJECTIVES The student will:

1. understand how to use the classified ads for a job search;

2. be able to write a letter of application for a job.

ACTIVITY 1 Review career clusters and check homework (students were to bring in a classified ad from the newspaper.) 10 minutes

ACTIVITY 2 Using the classified ads from the workbook, select two options. See "employment agent" (teacher) to make your selection. Glue job description into workbook. 25 minutes

ACTIVITY 3 Using real newspaper classified ads, complete "job hunt" worksheet to hand in. *Note:* Activities 2 and 3 will go on at same time.

ACTIVITY 4 Mini-lecture—writing a letter of application for a job. Handout— sample letter. 15 minutes

ACTIVITY 5 Student activity—Write a rough draft of a letter of application for the job selected in the workbook. Teacher will proofread and offer suggestions. Students will rewrite for homework. 38 minutes

Note: This course uses the workbook *Living on Your Own* by J. Weston Walch.

■ FAMILY AND CONSUMER SCIENCE

Jeanne Lamb
North East High School
North East, PA

INDEPENDENT LIVING: NUTRITION AND HEALTH

GRADE LEVEL   12
TYPE OF EXTENDED BLOCK   A/B trimester
NUMBER OF MINUTES PER CLASS   88

OBJECTIVES   The student will:

1. understand the relationship between calories and weight gain;

2. review the food groups in the food guide pyramid.

ACTIVITY 1   Discuss fitness, nutrition, and health, pages 2–7, *You* books, including activity on pages 5 and 7 to hand in.   30 minutes

ACTIVITY 2   Discussion of food guide pyramid.   15 minutes

ACTIVITY 3   Video: *The New Food Guide Pyramid*   25 minutes

ACTIVITY 4   Page 20 in book to hand in.   18 minutes

Source: This lesson uses the *You* books from the Dairy Council.

■ GENERAL SCIENCE

PROPERTIES OF MINERALS

TYPE OF EXTENDED BLOCK 4×4
NUMBER OF MINUTES PER CLASS 85

OBJECTIVES The student will:

1. list general properties of minerals;

2. categorize the properties of minerals;

3. write a summary of factual information about minerals.

ACTIVITY 1 Independent Task/Cooperative Learning   10 minutes

Students will brainstorm a list of what comes to mind when they think of the word *mineral*. After about three minutes, each group will then generate one group list with information gained.

ACTIVITY 2 Mini-lecture/Group Discussion   20 minutes

Teacher will lead students in the creation of the first part of a K-W-L chart, with students using the group lists they created. Teacher will then present a tray with minerals on them. As students look at the samples, the teacher will direct them in the development of the W part of the chart.

ACTIVITY 3 Guided Reading   25 minutes

Students will be directed in reading the "Mineral" chapter. During reading, teacher will stop to conduct class discussion on the important content. Students will be redirected to the K-W-L chart for progress check and clarification of information.

ACTIVITY 4 Independent Writing   15 minutes

Students will be directed to write a paragraph of five to seven sentences summarizing what information they have gained (that addresses the W areas of the K-W-L chart) in the class today.

ACTIVITY 5 Cooperative Learning   15 minutes

Students will meet in learning groups to share verbally their summaries. Groups will refer to the lists created at the beginning of class. Using each person's summary and the initial group list, and referring to the K-W-L chart, students will create one summary to submit for evaluation.

■ GEOGRAPHY

UPPER SOUTH REGION

GRADE LEVEL 9
ACADEMIC LEVEL Average
TYPE OF EXTENDED BLOCK 4 × 4
NUMBER OF MINUTES PER CLASS 80

OBJECTIVES The student will:

1. recall the seven states and capitals of the Upper South Region of the United States;

2. locate the states and capitals on a map;

3. document the agriculture, industries, and geographical features of these states.

ACTIVITY 1 Teacher-conducted review linking previous class information utilizing classroom map to review locations and names of New England states and the mid-Atlantic states.   5 minutes

ACTIVITY 2 Teacher projects map of Upper South Region. Students will fill in their own map after the teacher cues them to the various states' locations.   10 minutes

ACTIVITY 3 Small group activity—Students will be divided into groups of three. Each student in the group will be assigned to research the agriculture, industry, or geography for the state assigned utilizing materials provided by the teacher.   20 minutes

ACTIVITY 4 Each small group will develop a poster highlighting their research.   15 minutes

ACTIVITY 5 A study guide will be introduced by the teacher. As small groups present research to the class, all students will fill in the guide for future study and reference.   25 minutes

ACTIVITY 6 The teacher will highlight the key points introduced by the small groups.   5 minutes

Note: Collect worksheet and maps to be evaluated.

■ GERMAN

Cheri Dohmen
North East High School
North East, PA

GERMAN 1

GRADE LEVEL 9-12
TYPE OF EXTENDED BLOCK A/B trimester
NUMBER OF MINUTES PER CLASS 88

OBJECTIVES The student will:

1. be able to review vocabulary and structures through the use of game activity;

2. be able to recognize and use adverbs of frequency in complete German sentences;

3. be able to find out and discuss the various activities of their classmates using appropriate vocabulary and adverbs of frequency;

4. be able to practice oral proficiency through the use of student activity survey and responses.

ACTIVITY 1 Agenda—Teacher shares, either through written agenda on board or orally, the agenda of activities for the classroom that day so that students are aware of where class will be heading during the time allotted. — 5–8 minutes

ACTIVITY 2 Warm-up activity—baseball review game for subject–verb agreement (copy attached). — 35–40 minutes

ACTIVITY 3 Baseball game sentence analysis—When teams have completed the baseball game exercise, each team will put one set of base sentences on the board, and the class will analyze the sentences to determine if they are grammatically correct or not and if not, then why. The team sentence sheets will be collected after that and the remaining sentences will be used for extra credit or a homework grade. — 15–20 minutes

ACTIVITY 4 Introduce adverbs of frequency—The adverbs *meistens, immer, oft, manchmal, selten,* and *nie* will be introduced to the class in a lecture burst of approximately 10 minutes in length. Using questioning to determine what various students do in their free time, it is possible to practice the construction of context in oral activities. — 15–20 minutes

ACTIVITY 5 Student survey—Students will take a survey of the various activities of their classmates in order to determine what they like to do in their free time and how often they do it. Each student must talk to two other students in the class, get the information needed, and then return to their place. Their surveys are collected and will be used in the next class when they will report the results and a collective survey result sheet will be organized. — 10–15 minutes

ACTIVITY 6 Preview of next class—Remaining class time will be used to preview what will be done in the next class. — 5 minutes

■ PHYSICAL SCIENCE

Theresa English
Conneaut Lake High School
Conneaut Lake, PA

PHYSICAL AND CHEMICAL CHANGES

NUMBER OF MINUTES PER CLASS   85

OBJECTIVES   The student will:

1. define physical change;

2. define chemical change;

3. given examples, determine what type of change is occurring.

ACTIVITY 1   Notes on physical and chemical changes.   10 minutes

ACTIVITY 2   Pick a Spot activity. (A) Give each student three pieces of paper.   20 minutes
(B) Have them write *physical* on one, *chemical* on one, and *not sure*
on the last. (C) Give them an example of a change, such as melting
a candle. (D) Have students think for ten seconds. (E) Then have
them choose a card and hold it up. (F) When everyone is holding
up a card, ask them to go to the appropriate spot in the room
(predetermined by teacher). (G) Ask for explanations from each
group. (H) Allow students to change their minds. (I) Tell the
correct answer and have the students report to their seats.
(J) Repeat steps C–I for at least six examples.

ACTIVITY 3   Go over lab and have students highlight important information   10 minutes
and instructions.

ACTIVITY 4   Have students perform a lab on chemical and physical changes.   30–40 minutes

ACTIVITY 5   Close by going over the lab. Collect lab.   10–15 minutes

■ PHYSICS

Theresa English
Conneaut Lake High School
Conneaut Lake, PA

FRICTION

TYPE OF EXTENDED BLOCK 4×4
NUMBER OF MINUTES PER CLASS 85

OBJECTIVES   The student will:

1. define static and kinesthetic friction;

2. give examples of static and kinesthetic friction;

3. solve friction problems.

ACTIVITY 1   Lecture on static and kinesthetic friction.   15–20 minutes

ACTIVITY 2   Have the students get into groups of four. Give each student   10–15 minutes
three notecards to be labeled as either *static, kinesthetic,* or *pass.*
Ask students questions and have them write the answer on the
appropriate card. Give an example of static friction; give an
example of kinesthetic friction. Students may only use the
"pass" card twice. After they write the responses down, they
must share with the group. The group agrees or disagrees with
each answer and offers solutions to the ones they disagree to.
Repeat this procedure at least six times.

ACTIVITY 3   Show example problems on the board.   10–15 minutes

ACTIVITY 4   Have the students solve problems individually.   30 minutes

ACTIVITY 5   Check worksheet with group. All must agree on the answer. If   10 minutes
they don't agree, the group must reach a consensus by resolving
the problem and explaining it out loud.

■ SOCIAL STUDIES

Gregory Henning
Social Studies Education
Edinboro University of PA

U.S. HISTORY: IMMIGRATION

GRADE LEVEL   10
TYPE OF EXTENDED BLOCK 4×4 or A/B
NUMBER OF MINUTES PER CLASS   90

OBJECTIVES The student will:

1. discuss the major problems facing new immigrants coming to America;

2. define the term *diversity* as it applies to culture;

3. view and analyze the film *Immigration and Culture.*

ACTIVITY 1	Set induction—students will be asked to consider and react to the statement, "Describe an American."	5 minutes
ACTIVITY 2	The teacher will distribute a handout, *Our Diverse Nation,* taken from the Internet. Students will react orally to the handout.	15 minutes
ACTIVITY 3	The teacher presents a mini-lecture as an introduction to the film. The teacher will provide background information and introduce the film guide to accompany the film.	10 minutes
ACTIVITY 4	Students will view the film and complete the guide.	45 minutes
ACTIVITY 5	Teacher-led guided discussion with the film guide.	10 minutes
ACTIVITY 6	*Closure:* The teacher reintroduces the Bellringer. Any changes in student opinion as a result of the information presented in class will be discussed.	5 minutes

U.S. HISTORY: DEPRESSION OF 1893 AND RISE OF THE POPULIST PARTY

GRADE LEVEL   10
TYPE OF EXTENDED BLOCK   4 × 4 or A/B
NUMBER OF MINUTES PER CLASS   80

OBJECTIVES   The student will:

1. explain the concept of an economic depression and how it applies to the events leading up to the Depression of 1893;

2. discuss the gold-versus-silver debate;

3. compare the campaign styles of the candidates in the presidential election of 1896;

4. elaborate on the Populist movement decline.

ACTIVITY 1	Introductory activity—Students receive card stock paper and are asked to create their own money.	10 minutes
ACTIVITY 2	The teacher leads a discussion reinforcing the need for money in society.	10 minutes
ACTIVITY 3	The teacher conducts a mini-lecture on economic depression and the gold/silver standard.	25 minutes
ACTIVITY 4	Cooperative learning—Small groups complete the study guide focusing on the Campaign of 1896 and the Populist movement.	25 minutes
ACTIVITY 5	Large-group discussion led by the teacher to review and reinforce concepts introduced in the study guide.	15 minutes
ACTIVITY 6	Closure to check for understanding—students complete a Quick Write responding to the following: "Discuss the impact of the Depression of 1893 on the U.S. economy."	5 minutes

■ SOCIAL STUDIES

U.S. HISTORY: INVENTIONS

GRADE LEVEL 9
ACADEMIC LEVEL Basic
TYPE OF EXTENDED BLOCK 4×4
NUMBER OF MINUTES PER CLASS 85

OBJECTIVES   The student will:

1. state reasons why communication is important;

2. describe inventions of the late 1880s and explain the impact of these inventions on people's lives;

3. describe inventions of their lifetimes and explain advantages and disadvantages of those inventions.

ACTIVITY 1   Cooperative Learning   10 minutes

Students will play a game of "telephone" in two groups.
Following the game, teacher will lead students in a discussion
of difficulties that took place while listening to the message.
This will be tied to the initial invention of the telephone.

ACTIVITY 2   Mini-Lecture   20 minutes

Teacher will discuss important inventions of the past and how they
impacted people's lives. Teacher will explain the patent process.

ACTIVITY 3   Cooperative Learning   20 minutes

Working with a partner, students will complete a worksheet
reviewing lecture information.

ACTIVITY 4   Guided Reading   20 minutes

Students will read the corresponding section of their text as
teacher directs. After each section read, teacher will ask questions,
and students will discuss as a class. Following discussion of each
teacher-presented issue, students will write independent
responses summarizing information gained in the discussion.

ACTIVITY 5   Guided Review/Cooperative Learning   15 minutes

In small groups, students will follow the Roundrobin strategy to
share responses written previously. At this time, students may
edit their individual responses. Teacher will collect all responses
to be evaluated.

■ SOCIAL STUDIES

AMERICAN GOVERNMENT: THE FEDERAL JUDICIARY

GRADE LEVEL 11
ACADEMIC LEVEL Basic
TYPE OF EXTENDED BLOCK 4×4
NUMBER OF MINUTES PER CLASS 85

OBJECTIVES The student will:

1. list and describe the components of the federal judiciary;

2. draw logical conclusions about the federal judiciary ideas of past and present.

ACTIVITY 1 Mini-Lecture   10 minutes

As a class, students will brainstorm information they have about the federal judiciary. Responses will be written on the board by the teacher. As responses are given, teacher will supplement with appropriate information.

ACTIVITY 2 Guided Learning   20 minutes

Students will be given an outline of the components of the federal judiciary. Teacher will discuss important information about each component as students take notes on the outline.

ACTIVITY 3 Cooperative Learning   20 minutes

Students will use the Heads Together approach to investigate descriptions of the courts. As students offer information, teacher will place cards with the court names forming the federal judiciary on the board.

ACTIVITY 4 Guided Reading   20 minutes

Students will read their text, one section at a time. At the end of each section, the teacher will pose questions concerning information in that section. The class will discuss responses to the issues raised.

ACTIVITY 5 Cooperative Learning/Paired Writing   15 minutes

Students will be given a question: "Is the federal judiciary as important today as when the framers put it into the Constitution? Why do you think the framers felt it was important? Provide contemporary examples that demonstrate the importance of the federal judiciary to you."

158   *Copyright © 1999 by Allyn and Bacon.*

■ **SPANISH**

Megan Horn
Spanish Education
Edinboro University of PA

SPANISH I: DOLER

ACADEMIC LEVEL   Mixed
TYPE OF EXTENDED BLOCK 4×4
NUMBER OF MINUTES PER CLASS   85

OBJECTIVES   The student will:

1. exhibit ability to read and understand written Spanish by participating in cooperative activity and by answering the questions in the story handout;

2. listen attentively to mini-lecture about the verb *doler;*

3. exhibit understanding of the conjugation and use of *doler* by translating sentences;

4. exhibit understanding of the use of *doler* by using it when writing in journals;

5. demonstrate ability to create sentences about pictures of people who feel pain in different parts of their body.

ACTIVITY 1   Direct the students to form pairs; give each pair a story which contains the *doler* construction. The students will also be given questions to answer about the reading selection. The questions will be discussed as a group.   20 minutes

ACTIVITY 2   Give a short mini-lecture about the verb *doler,* focusing on how it is used and the construction in all of the present-tense verb forms. Use many examples and encourage the students to ask questions.   15 minutes

ACTIVITY 3   Give the students sentences in English to translate into Spanish. This will be done in class to ensure that the students understand the use and construction of *doler.* Then go over the sentences as a class.   15 minutes

ACTIVITY 4   Give the students twenty minutes to write in their Spanish journals. Direct them to write about the parts of their bodies that would hurt if they were in an accident.   20 minutes

ACTIVITY 5   Review the verb *doler* and check for understanding by showing pictures of stick figures in various types of pain and having the students tell in Spanish how the people are feeling. Have some drawings of only one person and some of more than one so that students have to use multiple verb forms.   15 minutes

■ SPANISH

Megan Horn
Spanish Education
Edinboro University of PA

SPANISH I: PARTS OF THE BODY

ACADEMIC LEVEL Mixed
TYPE OF EXTENDED BLOCK 4×4
NUMBER OF MINUTES PER CLASS 85

OBJECTIVES The student will:

1. identify orally and aurally twelve parts of the body by participating in the Total Physical Response (TPR) activity;

2. exhibit aural and oral understanding of ten parts of the body by creating flash cards from visuals;

3. describe uses for four parts of the body by generating simple sentences in a Think-Pair-Share cooperative learning activity;

4. demonstrate ability to identify certain parts of the body by pointing to them when given the Spanish word;

5. demonstrate understanding of new vocabulary by completing *"Les Partes del Cuerpo"* handout.

ACTIVITY 1 Using TPR, introduce the parts of the body. Point to each part of the body and say its name, directing the students to repeat it. After several repetitions, point to the part of the body and ask the students to give the name. | 15 minutes

ACTIVITY 2 After handing out blank flash cards, use visuals on the overhead projector to introduce the words again. Use an overlay to write the word next to the body part. The students will write the English words on one side of the flash cards. Ask the students to give the Spanish word, which they will write on the other side of the flash card. The Spanish names for the body parts will also be written on the overlay. | 15 minutes

ACTIVITY 3 Use a Think-Pair-Share activity to discuss the uses for different body parts. Write four body parts on the board and direct the students to generate sentences describing a use for each body part. Put a word bank on the overhead projector to assist the students in creating sentences. The students will form pairs and will read their partner's responses. The students will then share all of their responses with the class. | 25 minutes

ACTIVITY 4 Have the students work on a teacher-developed handout that reviews the body parts and their uses. | 20 minutes

ACTIVITY 5   Direct the students to recite the name of the body part being   10 minutes
pointed at by the teacher. Ask individual students to pick body
parts at which to point. Go around the class and have one student
point at a body part and then another student give the Spanish
word. All students will need to supply the Spanish word at least
once.

■ References

American Association for the Advancement of Science. (1989). *Science for all Americans: Project 2061 report on goals in science, mathematics, and technology.* Washington, DC: Author.

Aronson, E., Blaney, N., Stephan, C., Sikes, J., & Snapp, M. (1978). *The jigsaw classroom.* Beverly Hills, CA: Sage Publications.

Auten, C. (1995, March 12). Questions about modular scheduling. [On-line] Available: Newsgroups: nptn.teacher.professional.

Averett, C. P. (1994). *Block scheduling in North Carolina high schools.* Raleigh: North Carolina Department of Public Instruction.

Bamberg, B. (1981, October). Composition in the secondary English curriculum. *Research in the Teaching of English, 15,* 257–266.

Bateson, D. J. (1990). Science achievement in semester and all-year courses. *Journal of Research in Science Teaching, 3,* 233–240.

Baxter, J. (1996). *Integrated Mathematics I: Transformational geometry.* Unpublished lesson plan outline.

Baxter, J. (1997). *Algebra II: Quadratic equations.* Unpublished lesson plan outline.

Baxter, J. (1997). *Teaching in the extended block.* Presentation at Student Teacher Practicum, Edinboro University of PA, March 11, 1997.

Bevevino, M. (1997, Fall). Writing projects: Taking teachers through the looking glass. Edited by E. H. Thompson. *Virginia English Bulletin, 47*(2), 122–127.

Bonwell, C. C., & Eison, J. A. (1991). *Active learning: Creating excitement in the classroom. ASHE-ERIC Higher Education Report No. 1.* Washington, DC: The George Washington University.

Braddock, R., et al. (1963). *Research in written composition.* Urbana, IL: National Council of Teachers of English.

Brett, M. (1996, February). Teaching extended class periods. *Social Education, 60*(2), 77–79.

Bybee, R., & Sund, R. (1990). *Piaget for educators.* Prospect Heights, IL: Waveland Press.

Canady, R. L., & Rettig, M. D. (1995). *Block scheduling: A catalyst for change in high schools.* Princeton, NJ: Eye on Education.

Canady, R. L., & Rettig, M. D. (1995, November). The power of innovative scheduling. *Educational Leadership, 55*(3), 4–10.

Carnes, W. J. (1995, November). Unleashing the Kraken: The perils of ignoring community values. *Educational Leadership, 55*(3), 84–86.

Cawelti, G. (1994). *High school restructuring: A national study.* Arlington, VA: Educational Research Service.

Collette, A., & Chiapetta, E. (1994). *Science instruction in the middle and secondary schools.* New York: Macmillan.

Cooney, T. J., & Hirsch, C. R. (1990). *Teaching and learning mathematics in the 1990s: 1990 yearbook.* Reston, VA: National Council of Teachers of Mathematics.

Cooper, J. M. (Ed.). (1990). *Classroom teaching skills* (4th ed.). Lexington, MA: D. C. Heath.

Danks, C. (1996, May–June). Using the literature of Elie Wiesel and selected poetry to teach the Holocaust in the secondary school history classroom. *The Social Studies, 87*(3), 101–105.

Davey, B. (1986). Using textbook activity guides to help students learn from textbooks. *Journal of Reading, 29,* 489–494.

Dohman, C. (1997). *German I.* Unpublished lesson plan outline.

Driscoll, M. (1982). *Research within reach: Secondary school mathematics.* Reston, VA: National Council of Teachers of Mathematics.

Edwards, C. M., Jr. (1995, November). The 4 × 4 plan. *Educational Leadership, 55*(3), 16–19.

English, T. (1997). *Physical science: Physical and chemical change.* Unpublished lesson plan outline.

English, T. (1997). *Physics: Friction*. Unpublished lesson plan outline.

Gore, G. R. (1997, January). 1996 provincial exam results and timetable. [On-Line]. Available: *Catalyst, 39*(3).

Graham, D. (1997). *English literature: History and music of the 1930s—Interdisciplinary concept stations*. Unpublished lesson plan outline.

Graves, M., Cooke, C., & Laberge, M. (1983). Effects of previewing difficult short stories on low ability junior high students' comprehension, recall, and attitudes. *Reading Research Quarterly, 18*, 262–276.

Hackmann, D. G. (1995, November). Ten guidelines for implementing block scheduling. *Educational Leadership, 55*(3), 24–27.

Hamdy, M., & Urich, T. (1998, March). Perceptions of teachers in South Florida toward block scheduling. *NASSP Bulletin, 82*(596), 79–82.

Hayes, D. A. (1989). Helping students GRASP the knack of writing summaries. *Journal of Reading, 32*, 96–101.

Haynes, E. (1978, January). Using research in preparing to teach writing. *English Journal, 67*, 82–88.

Henning, G. (1997). *U.S. History: Immigration*. Unpublished lesson plan outline.

Hillocks, G. (1986). *Research on written composition*. Urbana, IL: National Council of Teachers of English, ERIC.

Horn, M. (1997). *Spanish I: Doler*. Unpublished lesson plan outline.

Horn, M. (1997). *Spanish I: Parts of the body*. Unpublished lesson plan outline.

Hottenstein, D. (1998, April). An "unobjective" look at "objective" math research involving block scheduling: A letter from David Hottenstein. *NASSP Bulletin, 82*(597), 117–119.

Hottenstein, D., & Malatesta, C. (1993). Putting a school in gear with intensive scheduling. *High School Magazine, 2*, 23–29.

International Reading Association and the National Council of Teachers of English. (1996). *Standards for the English language arts*. Urbana, IL: Authors.

Johnson, D. W., & Johnson, R. T. (1989). *Cooperating and competition: Theory and research*. Edina, MN: Interaction Book Company.

Johnson, D. W., & Johnson, R. T. (1991). *Learning together and alone* (3rd ed.). Englewood Cliffs, NJ: Prentice-Hall.

Joyce, B., Neil, M., & Showers, B. (1992). *Models of teaching*. Boston: Allyn and Bacon.

Kagan, S. (1985). *Cooperative learning resources for teachers*. Spencer Kagan, Department of Psychology, University of California at Riverside, Riverside, CA 92521.

Karplus, R., et al. (1977). *Teaching and the development of reasoning*. Berkeley: University of California Press.

Kelmickis, K. (1997). *English: Poe's Fall of the House of Usher*. Unpublished lesson plan outline.

Kemp, C. (1997). *American literature: Emily Dickinson*. Unpublished lesson plan outline.

Kemp, C. (1997). *Basic English: The mystery novel*. Unpublished lesson plan outline.

Kramer, S. L. (1996, December). Block scheduling and high school mathematics instruction. *The Mathematics Teacher, 89*(9), 758–768.

Kramer, S. L. (1997, February). What we know about block scheduling and its effects on math instruction, Part I. *NASSP Bulletin, 81*(586), 18–42.

Kramer, S. L. (1997, March). What we know about block scheduling and its effects on math instruction, Part II. *NASSP Bulletin, 81*(587), 69–82.

Lamb, J. (1997). *Family and consumer science: Food preparation—Italian cuisine*. Unpublished lesson plan outline.

Lamb, J. (1997). *Family and consumer science: Food preparation—Restaurant project*. Unpublished lesson plan outline.

Lamb, J. (1997). *Family and consumer science: Food preparation—Safety and measuring equipment*. Unpublished lesson plan outline.

Lamb, J. (1997). *Family and consumer science: Foods 3—Menu planning*. Unpublished lesson plan outline.

Lamb, J. (1997). *Family and consumer science: Independent living—Employment*. Unpublished lesson plan outline.

Lamb, J. (1997). *Family and consumer science: Independent living—Nutrition and health*. Unpublished lesson plan outline.

Langer, J. A. (Ed.). (1992). *Literature instruction: A focus on student response*. Urbana, IL: National Council of Teachers of English

Lawson, A. (1995). *Science teaching and the development of thinking*. Belmont, CA: Wadsworth.

Legler, E. (1997). *Child development: Planning for a baby*. Unpublished lesson plan outline.

Legler, E. (1997). *Career planning: Career choices*. Unpublished lesson plan outline.

Lyman, F. (1981). The responsive classroom discussion. In A. S. Anderson (Ed.), *Mainstreaming digest*. College Park: University of Maryland College of Education.

Manhood, W., Biemer, L., & Lowe, W. T. (1991). *Teaching social studies in middle and senior high schools*. New York: Merrill.

Marshall, M., Taylor, A., Bateson, D., & Brigden, S. (1995). *The British Columbia assessment of mathematics and science: Preliminary report* (draft). Victoria: British Columbia Ministry of Education.

Martorella, P. H. (1991). *Teaching social studies in middle and secondary schools*. New York: Macmillan, Inc.

Maxwell, R. J., & Meiser, M. J. (1997). *Teaching English in middle and secondary schools* (2nd ed.). Upper Saddle River, NJ: Merrill.

Mechlinger, H. D. (1992, March). "The National Commission on social studies in the schools: An example of the politics of curriculum reform in the United States." *Social Education, 56*(3), 149–153.

Miller, K. (1997). *English: Creative writing*. Unpublished lesson plan outline.

Miller, K. (1997). *English: Creative writing and point of view*. Unpublished lesson plan outline.

Milligan, N. (1997). *Economics: Starting a new business*. Unpublished lesson plan outline.

Milner, J. B., & Milner, L. F. M. (1993). *Bridging English*. New York: Merrill.

Mulligan, A. (1997). Personal communication.

National Commission on Excellence in Education. (1983). *A nation at risk: The imperative for educational reform. A report to the nation and the Secretary of Education*. Washington, DC: Author.

National Commission on Time and Learning. (1994). *Prisoners of time*. Washington, DC: Author.

National Council of Teachers of English. (1995). *Teaching the writing process in high school: Standards consensus series*. Urbana, IL: Author.

National Council of Teachers of English. (1996). *Motivating writing in middle school: Standards consensus series*. Urbana, IL: Author.

National Council of Teachers of Mathematics. (1996, September). *Building block or stumbling block? A look at block scheduling in mathematics education: News bulletin*. [On-line].

National Council of Teachers of Mathematics Commission on Standards for School Mathematics. (1989). *Curriculum and evaluation standards for school mathematics*. Reston, VA: Author.

National Council for the Social Studies. (1994). *Expectations of excellence: Curriculum standards for social studies*. Reston, VA: Author.

National Research Council. (1995). *National science education standards*. Washington, DC: Author.

National Science Teachers Association. (1992). *Scope, sequence and coordination of secondary school science*. Washington, DC: Author.

Nauman, D. (1997). *English: Elements of a story*. Unpublished lesson plan outline.

Nauman, D. (1997). *English: The short story*. Unpublished lesson plan outline.

Needham, N. R. (1993, April). Radical restructuring: Changing school culture. *NEA Today, 11*(8), 15.

Nogachi, R. (1991). *Grammar and the teaching of writing*. Urbana, IL: National Council of Teachers of English.

Ogle, D. (1986). KWL: A teaching model that develops active reading of expository text. *The Reading Teacher, 39*, 564–570.

Oliver, D., & Shaver, J. P. (1966). *Teaching public issues in the high school*. Boston: Houghton Mifflin.

O'Neil, J. (1995, November). Finding time to learn. *Educational Leadership, 53*(3),11–15.

Open house will explain system. (1996, December 3). *The Standard-Times*, New Bedford, MA, pp. B1–B2.

Parents for Academic Excellence. (1997). *Block scheduling house of problems.* [On-line] Available: block.scheduling@poboxes.com.

Picciotto, H. (1995). *Structuring time.* [On-line] Available: hot@SOE.Berkeley.Edu.

Plyler, D. (1997). *English: Note taking.* Unpublished lesson plan outline.

Postamentier, A. S., & Stepelman, J. (1995). *Teaching secondary school mathematics: Techniques and enrichment units* (4th ed.). Englewood Cliffs, NJ: Prentice-Hall.

Queen, J. A., Algozzine, R. F., & Eaddy, M. A. (1996, November–December). The success of 4 × 4 block scheduling. *The Social Studies, 87*(6), 249–253.

Rettig, M. D., & Canady, R. L. (1998, March). High failure rates in required mathematics courses: Can a modified block schedule be part of the cure? *NASSP Bulletin, 82*(596), 56–65.

Rodriquez-McCleary, B., & Vaught, M. J. (1994). *Anticipation prediction guide.* Fairfax, VA: Fairfax County Schools.

Salvaterra, M., & Adams, D. (1995, November). Departing from tradition: Two schools' stories. *Educational Leadership, 53*(3), 32–35.

Scaletta, J. (1997). *AP calculus: The decay process.* Unpublished lesson plan outline.

Scaletta, R. (1997, August). Personal communication.

Schoenstein, R. (1994, Spring). *Restructuring pitfalls.* [On-line] Available: rajscho@rmii.com.

Schwab, J. (1965). Invitations to enquiry. In *Biological sciences curriculum study: Biology teacher's handbook.* New York: Wiley.

Seta, J. J., Paulus, P. B., & Schkade, J. K. (1976). Effects of group size and proximity under cooperative and competitive conditions. *Journal of Personality and Social Psychology, 34,* 47–53.

Shara, S., Ackerman, Z., & Hertz-Lazarowitz, R. (1980). Academic achievement of elementary school children in small groups vs. whole class instruction. *Journal of Experimental Education,* 125–129.

Shaver, J. P. (1992, May–June). Rationale for issues-centered social studies education. *The Social Studies, 83*(3), 95–99.

Singer, A., Dircks, H., & Turner, V. (1996, September). Exploring the Great Depression and the New Deal. *Social Education, 60*(5), C1–C4.

Slavin, R. E. (1986). *Using student team learning: The Johns Hopkins Team Learning Project* (3rd ed.). Baltimore, MD: The Johns Hopkins University.

Slavin, R. E. (1987). *Cooperative learning: Student teams* (2nd ed.). Washington, DC: National Education Association.

Slavin, R. E. (1987). Cooperative learning and the cooperative school. *Educational Leadership, 45,* 7–13.

Slavin, R. E. (1995). *Cooperative learning* (2nd ed.). Boston: Allyn and Bacon.

Shaughnessy, M. (1977). *Errors and expectations.* New York: Oxford University Press.

Smagorinsky, P. (1990). Developing a social conscience through literature. In P. Phelan (Ed.), *Literature and life: Making connections in the classroom* (pp. 13–18). Urbana, IL: National Council of Teachers of English.

Smagorinsky, P. (1996). *Standards in practice: Grades 9–12.* Urbana, IL: National Council of Teachers of English.

Stumpf, T. (1995, November). A Colorado school's un-rocky road to trimesters. *Educational Leadership, 53*(3), 20–22.

Suchman, R. J. (1962). *The elementary school training program in scientific inquiry. Report to the U.S. Office of Education, Project VII.* Urbana: University of Illinois.

Sullivan, J. (1996, September–October). Implementing a cooperative learning research model: How it applies to a real social studies unit. *The Social Studies, 87*(5), 210–216.

Toepfer, C. F., Jr. (1990, January). Heterogeneous grouping in middle level schools: Leadership responsibilities for principals. National Association of Secondary School Principals, *Schools in the middle: A report on trends and practices,* pp. 1–4.

Trowbridge, L. & Bybee, R. (1990). *Becoming a secondary school science teacher.* New York: Merrill.

Watkins, A. (1997). *English: American poetry.* Unpublished lesson plan outline.

Waychoff, J. (1997). *Algebra I: Linear equations.* Unpublished lesson plan outline.

Willis, S. (1995). *Reinventing science education curriculum update, summer 1–8.* Alexandria, VA: Association for Supervision and Curriculum Development.

Wilson, C. (1995). The 4 × 4 block system: A workable alternative. *NASSP Bulletin, 79*(571), 63–66.

Wood, K. D. (1987). Helping readers comprehend their textbook. *Middle School Journal, 18*(2), 20–21.

Wood, K. D. (1992). Fostering collaborative reading and writing experiences in mathematics. *Journal of Reading, 36*(2), 96–103.

Worthen, C. (1997). *English: Personal essay.* Unpublished lesson plan outline.

Yonko, K. (1997). *Biology: Animal kingdoms.* Unpublished lesson plan outline.

Yonko, K. (1997). *Ecology: Endangered species.* Unpublished lesson plan outline.

■ Index